SHATTERED
DREAM

SHATTERED DREAM

America's Search for Its Soul

WALTER T. DAVIS, JR.

TRINITY PRESS INTERNATIONAL
Valley Forge, Pennsylvania

For
Libby, Trae, Laura, Martha, and Lamar,
my closest companions in the search
for a new dream.

First Published 1994

Trinity Press International
P.O. Box 851
Valley Forge, PA 19482–0851

Cover Design by Jim Gerhard
Cover Photo by Chris Usher

The poem on p. vii is from *Collected Poems* by W. H. Auden © 1940 and renewed 1968 by W. H. Auden. Reprinted by permission of Random House, Inc.

Library of Congress Cataloging-in-Publication Data

Davis, Walter T.
    Shattered dream : America's search for its soul / Walter T. Davis, Jr.
      p.   cm.
    Includes bibliographical references and index.
    ISBN 1-56338-095-1
    1. United States—Civilization—1970– 2. Vietnamese Conflict, 1961–75—Influence. 3. United States—History — Religious aspects—Christianity.   I. Title.
E169.12.D364 1994
973.92–dc20   94–10248
                                        CIP

Printed in the United States of America

94   95   96   97   98   99   10 9 8 7 6 5 4 3 2 1

Contents

Preface

Follow, poet, follow right
To the bottom of the night,
With your unconstraining voice
Still persuade us to rejoice;

With the farming of a verse
Make a vineyard of the curse,
Sing of human unsuccess
In a rapture of distress;

In the deserts of the heart
Let the healing fountain start,
In the prison of his days
Teach the free man how to praise.

—W. H. Auden,
"In Memory of W. B. Yeats"

As a nation we have lost our way. We do not know where we are going because we no longer know who we are. We no longer know who we are because the stories we have lived by no longer make sense. The roots of our condition reach down into the very origins of our existence as a people, but the crisis erupted a quarter of a century ago when our projected self-image, a larger-than-life representation of generations of American heroes, died in Vietnam. It was the greatest loss we have suffered as a nation.

The Vietnam War left us polarized and exhausted. First in Grenada, then in Panama, and more recently in the Persian Gulf, our leaders have sought to "put Vietnam behind us" without examining the nature of our loss or how its legacy infects every dimension of our current domestic malaise. Like a patient with a tumor who prefers to deny the illness rather than undergo painful treatment, we have repressed that legacy. While a few prophets describe us as a culture in decline and a people at war with each other, or even a nation in exile, our leaders pretend that little has changed at a fundamental level.[1] Meanwhile, the malignancy spreads.

One group of Americans has faced the illness and probed its meaning. This group is the war veterans themselves, especially the poets and novelists among them. As part of their own personal therapy they have traveled "right to the bottom of the night." For them this has been a life-or-death struggle to make sense of personal experience as well as national trauma. At bottom, theirs is a religious pilgrimage in search of faith, hope, and love. Having lost their faith in God, country, and self, and finding themselves without hope, many veterans have turned to literature and poetry in order to recover a love for life, a source for praise.

This book explores the underlying causes of contemporary national decay through the hermeneutical lens of their experience, for they are bearers of revelation. Until we come to terms with their apocalypse, we as a nation will flounder without clear identity or purpose. Here then is an interpretive guide that suggests ways in which religious communities can contribute to a new vision of America in the light of what these secular theologians have to teach us.

Research for This Book

While James Michener was writing his thirty-third book, *Texas,* he told a reporter: "When it comes to research, I'm a total-immersion Baptist. I believe you can't make it unless you get right down into the middle of the river. So I live in the state, read its papers, listen to its radio stations, go to its football games. I'm trying to be a Texan." In the spirit of Michener's example, I have attempted, insofar as possible, to get inside the combat soldier's experience. At first I launched into a series of interviews with a wide variety of vets, until I realized that no matter how systematic my interview schedule, the interviews became impressionistic and anecdotal. When vets try to put their experiences into an overall framework, they invariably turn to film and literature. This discovery led me to alternate intensive interviews with concentrated study of cinema and literature.

A sabbatical leave from teaching and administration at San Francisco Theological Seminary allowed me to interview vets in different parts of the country and to spend long periods of total immersion in the literature. Particularly helpful was a sojourn at Colorado State University where Professors John Clark Pratt and John Newman have gathered a complete special collection of Vietnam War fiction.

Professor Pratt pointed me to the most relevant literature. Extended conversations with him helped focus the major thesis of this work and provided new impetus for another round of interviews with chaplains, "grunts" (foot soldiers), nurses, "lifers" (career officers), PTSD (post–traumatic stress disorder) therapists, vet center directors, Veterans Administration medical center personnel, and authors and professors who write and teach about the war. Visits to local chapter meetings of Vietnam Veterans of America and the National Conference of Vietnam Veteran Ministers have been supplemented by interviews with antiwar activists and veterans from earlier wars. In the midst of this research process, I have taught courses on the war to a variety of groups including graduate students at the Graduate Theological Union and clergy engaged in the Advanced Pastoral Studies program at San Francisco Theological Seminary. One of my most interesting and challenging teaching roles involved a course taught in the fall of 1990 at the Redwood City Public Library, sponsored by the National Endowment for the Humanities. The participants included a cross section of citizens ranging from gung ho superpatriots to disillusioned veterans, from antiwar activists to Nixon loyalists, from pro-Saigon refugees to Ho Chi Minh sympathizers. In early 1992 I spent a month in Cambodia and Vietnam gaining a different perspective on the war, seventeen years after the fall of Saigon.

Methodology

At every stage of the work I have been attentive to the suggestion of Kurt Lewin that there is nothing more practical than a good theory. Theories act like a microscope or telescope, bringing into focus that which otherwise is not clearly seen. Theories may also act like metal detectors, telling us where to look. Then again, they may act like the lenses of sunglasses, filtering out certain rays of light so that the rich textures and colors of the world can be seen in sharper contrast. At the same time, they may block out parts of reality that could be visible to us were we not so wedded to the selective vision they provide. Thus, theory and experience are like the negative and positive poles of a magnet, always in tension with each other, the one being informed by and at the same time corrected by the other. In each chapter I have attempted to maintain a dialectical conversation between the two, as applied to different dimensions of the war.

No attempt has been made to test any a priori theory. Nor is there an effort to fit all the various concepts into an overall theoretical perspective. Rather, I have approached the selection of appropriate theory inductively, allowing the narrative material itself to suggest appropriate conceptual lenses. The result is a somewhat eclectic collage of concepts that seem coherent with each other even if they do not form a neat, overall, explanatory framework. Figure 1 depicts the relationship of the various concepts to each other, though the journey of any particular veteran probably involves a much more confused pattern of false directions, spiraling repetitions, and backward as well as forward movements.

No claim is made that all vets have followed or should follow this same journey. My selective interpretation of

Figure 1
RITE OF PASSAGE

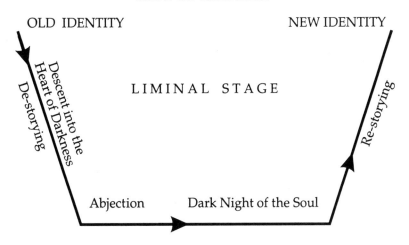

oral and literary sources traces the journey of some vets. My claim is that the journey outlined here is the most profound and the most revelatory for the nation as a whole.

Two further comments are necessary regarding the selection of experiences to be examined. First, this work is about the American experience in Vietnam, and only indirectly about the experience of Vietnamese and other peoples of the region. The danger of this approach is a reinforcement of the popular meaning of "Vietnam," which has become a synonym for American wounds, to the near-total neglect of the far greater price paid by the Vietnamese, Cambodians, and other peoples of Southeast Asia. We still have no memorial that acknowledges the suffering inflicted upon the inhabitants of the region. Nevertheless, in addition to the obvious limits of length, there is another justification for limiting the focus to the American experience. We are now in a position to understand that "long before most Americans even knew that Vietnam existed,

we had imagined 'Vietnams' of many sorts."[2] Only by
probing the American experience in depth, and discovering how our historic identity contributed almost inevitably
to such a disaster, will we be able to revise the meaning of
America and alter our purpose in the world so that new
"Vietnams" can be prevented.

Second, this book is limited mainly to the experiences
of selected American *men* of European descent who served
in Vietnam. While it is true that many more men than
women served there (three million men versus eleven
thousand women), the women who did serve had experiences of equal terror and trauma. Because the majority
of the women were nurses serving in hospitals in battle
zones — almost the entire country was a battle zone at one
time or another — they experienced trauma disproportion-
ate to their numbers. Women, however, were less invested
than men in the classic search for machismo required by
the American national narrative. Thus the descent into the
heart of darkness and journey through the dark night of
the soul carried different nuances and implications for men
than for women. In short, what was at stake in this war
was the traditional definition of manliness. By focusing on
white men, the primary carriers of the dominant American narrative, I have tried to show the importance of the
shattering of that narrative for the changing relationships
between racial groups and between men and women in
contemporary American society.

Acknowledgments

My greatest debt is to those Vietnam veterans whose stories provide the inspiration for this book. Those whose
stories are in print are mentioned throughout the text, but
the names of scores of oral informants must be withheld,
to respect their request for anonymity. In addition to these,
I wish to express appreciation to the following people
who contributed to the shaping of the argument devel-

oped in this book: Lily Adams, Gene Allen, Walter Capps, Gary Cox, John Durham, Con Edwards, John Fergueson, Linda Hedges, Dick Heim, Bill Herod, Phil Kinsey, Maceo May, Dick McGonnigal, Bruce Murphy, Ninh Nguyen, John Phalen, Steve Pennington, Jim Quay, Rose Sandecki, Sarah Sheehan, Rick Thomas, and Dick Walenta. John Newman, Alice Spaulding, and Michael Peterson proved to be expert sleuths in chasing down every imaginable bibliographical source.

I am particularly grateful to those who offered critical evaluations of earlier drafts of the manuscript: Walter Brueggemann, Barbara Chasman, Barbara Cheatham (whose M.A. thesis and personal encouragement initiated my teaching and research in this area), Emory Cowan, Libby, Martha, and Trae Davis, Roy Fairchild, Rolland Fletcher, John Hadsell, Jim Johnson, Kermit Johnson, Margaret Keyes, Bill Mahedy, Lew Mudge, Kathryn Poethig, John Pratt, Mike Stuart, and Randy Taylor. A careful reading by such a diverse group of friendly critics ensures that the author must make painful decisions among conflicting interpretations. Although none of these critics will be completely satisfied with my interpretive decisions, I trust that each will find merit in the overall argument.

Laura Barrett (Managing Editor) and Harold Rast (Publisher) of Trinity Press International are an author's wish fulfilled, a wonderful blend of strategist, cheerleader, and critic. Copy editor Hank Schlau decisively improved the style of the text, and John Eagleson did fine work as the designer and typesetter.

Special mention is due the following persons: my colleagues in the Advanced Pastoral Studies Office of San Francisco Theological Seminary; Warren Lee, who covered for me during periods of intense off-campus research; Patricia Perry, whose expert editing of four versions of the manuscript greatly improved its accuracy and coherence; Dean Lewis Mudge, whose example, support, and encouragement of SFTS faculty scholarship is unparalleled; and James P. Johnson, who, as a congressman (R. Colorado), fought the war in Washington and, as a trustee of SFTS, offered valuable encouragement throughout my research. Finally, I give thanks for W. H. Auden's reminder in the poem that begins this work (p. vii) that even in the darkest of days the common vocation of all who would build communities of hope is to teach the art of praise.

Introduction

Vietnam is the place where everybody finds out who
they are.
                    —Robert Stone, *Dog Soldiers*

Vision Gridlock

The 1992 presidential campaign gave voice to widespread
anxiety over the *economic* future of the nation. Bill Clinton
won the election on his promise to recover the American
Dream. This same economic anxiety animates the public
debate between the prophets of decline and the advocates
of renewal. The latter point to the end of the cold war,
the victory of capitalism, and more recently the prospects
of peace in the Middle East; the former cite the national
deficit, decline in productivity and the standard of living, environmental degradation, and social decay; but the
same underlying crises give rise to both sides of the debate.
Book titles like *The End of the American Century* and *Beyond
American Hegemony* provoke such ideological opposites as
America's Economic Resurgence and *The Myth of America's Decline*.[1] Other writers, like Clinton's deputy director of the
Office of Management and Budget, Alice M. Rivlin, who
has just written *Reviving the American Dream*,[2] take a me-
diating position that combines the hopes of the optimists
and the fears of the pessimists.

The nation faces a number of interrelated crises, each
with an economic dimension: inadequate health care, poor
education, joblessness, homelessness, the working poor,
environmental stress, resource depletion, urban decay and
unrest, racism and interethnic conflict, infrastructure deterioration, an increase in violence and fear. The list goes

on. The "new world order" that President Bush proclaimed looks less stable in some ways than the superpower rivalry it replaced. Most frustrating of all, the old solutions — money, science, technology, "can-do" optimism — no longer seem effective.

Political historian Paul Kennedy notes that a similar crisis in Western societies occurred just as the industrial revolution began. At that time poverty, crime, and social unrest threatened the fabric of those societies. Massive societal breakdown was prevented by emigration, an increase in food production, and labor-enhancing manufacturing technology, solutions that merely exacerbate our problems today. Britain, the leading world power then, chose to answer the decline/renewal debate of the time with a policy of muddling through. Should the United States attempt the same today, notes Kennedy, the results would be similar: "slow, steady, relative *decline*."[3]

Although the American Dream involves an entire way of life, not just material affluence, it is appropriate to focus on the economic dimensions of the dream because they provide the lubricant for other aspects of that way of life. Certainly the dominant narrative that I will identify in a later chapter as "American Exceptionalism" could not have developed historically had the material conditions been unfavorable. Now that these conditions are changing, the question arises: How well will we be able to preserve other ideals of the American narrative — democratic process, equality of opportunity, civil rights and civil liberties, a haven for the poor and oppressed, as well as corrective justice for victims of race, gender, and class discrimination? If the gap between ideal and reality is so great during conditions of abundance, how wide will the gap grow during conditions of scarcity?

Bill Clinton won the election because of "the economy, Stupid," and the nation rightfully focuses on economic issues because they are instrumental to the achievement of other goals. However, few informed people believe that our ills are limited to the economy. Although economic and fiscal matters take center stage, along with political gridlock, many recognize a larger *cultural* dimension to our predicament, what may be called *vision gridlock*. In this regard Mr. Clinton's promise of "change" is disappointing, for it is empty of any evocative, metaphorical substance. No matter how much Clinton admires John F. Kennedy, the narrative that gave rise to "Camelot" and the "New Frontier" no longer generates images of an alluring future. What we need most — a persuasive, modified narrative with power to draw us into the future — our leaders are least able to provide.

A national narrative does more than define a people; it also provides the vision of an anticipated future. We not only live *out of* our story; we also live *into* our story. What we shall become is always prefigured by what we have been. The history we recount directs us toward the future prescribed within it. When the interpretation of our past is altered, the imagined scenario that draws us into the future also undergoes change. As a nation we are in an analogous position to Vietnam vets. Although our narrative has been "de-storied" by that war and by the subsequent economic and social decline, we have yet to "re-story" our collective journey.

Since the self is structured in conversation with society, reconstruction of the narratives of individual vets calls for collective narrative reconstruction. The corollary also applies: collective narrative reconstruction requires that we as a nation come to terms with the de-storying experience of the Vietnam vets. We will not be able to look forward creatively until we have looked back caringly and come to terms with the legacy of that war.

Cultural War: A Crisis of National Identity

The American war in Vietnam was really a civil war, "the American Civil War of the twentieth century fought twelve thousand miles away."[4] It divided the nation like nothing else since the 1860s. When the troops returned and Saigon fell to the communists in 1975, we turned our backs on the region and on the veterans who had fought there.

Four years later Iranian students took Americans hostage in Tehran. When President Carter's rescue mission exploded in the desert, a newspaper columnist pondered: "Ah, John Wayne, where were you in Iran's desert?...The mission was as clear and good as John Wayne's on Iwo Jima beach. Americans were there to save innocent Americans held illegal captives by terrorists from a third-rate country spitting in our face....John Wayne is what we are all about. At least, what we thought we were all about."[5]

By the time Ronald Reagan was elected president in November 1980, our national pride had reached its nadir, plummeting steadily to the cadence of Walter Cronkite's nightly reminder: "That's the way it is today,...the 40th day,...the 100th day,...the 175th day,...the 269th day of captivity for the Americans in Iran." The Reagan presidency was dedicated to the restoration of American honor by "standing tall." President Reagan broke with the policies of "détente" and "containment," which his predecessors had pursued; instead, he declared Vietnam "a noble cause" and adopted a "rollback" policy, illustrated best by direct U.S. intervention in Grenada and Lebanon, by the bombing of Libya, and by U.S. support for the low-intensity conflict of the contras in Nicaragua. Thus began another phase of the twentieth-century American civil war, a battle for control of the national memory.[6]

In late January 1991, shortly before the ground war began in the Persian Gulf, *Time* essayist Charles Krauthammer wrote: "What's at stake in the Gulf War is the Vietnam legacy....In Vietnam, was America defeated by a constellation of contingencies...or did it succumb to itself, to overweening ambition and moral blindness, to a refusal to acknowledge its own mortality and limits?"[7] After the ground war, President Bush exclaimed in his radio message to American troops: "The specter of Vietnam has been buried forever in the desert sands of the Arabian Peninsula!"

Desert Storm was certainly different from the U.S. military campaign in Vietnam. The enemy was clearly identifiable, and the objectives were obvious. There were no drugs or indiscipline, no "fraggings" of unpopular officers.[8] Desert Storm put Americans into their accustomed role of waging a righteous war on behalf of the weak against a cruel and evil dictator. All over America yellow ribbons and national flags decorated homes, businesses, vehicles, and personal clothing. Instead of condemnation, the troops received an abundance of supportive mail from people they did not know. After the war, some commentators cautioned against renewed arrogance, but most welcomed the restoration of national pride and military confidence. Newspapers and magazines carried stories of jubilant officers with a message: "We're still Number One! The U.S. armed forces are the finest in the world — in the history of the world! Let the world take notice! When you provoke the U.S., watch out!" Some policy analysts claimed that the Gulf War "culminated a struggle in which the cultural and political ideology of the Ronald Reagan era routed its liberal critics as decisively as the Allied forces routed Iraq's Republican Guard."[9]

On March 6, 1991, just following the end of hostilities in the Persian Gulf, a political cartoon by Tom Meyer appeared in the *San Francisco Chronicle* (see fig. 2). Clearly more was at stake in the Gulf War than defeating Saddam Hussein and reinstating the Kuwaiti royal family. For the Bush administration the restoration of American self-confidence was perhaps even more important. In this light the cartoon is ambiguous. It could mean that because the Vietnam syndrome is buried forever in the Arabian desert, we need no longer explore its meaning. On the other hand, it could mean that the "Gulf War syndrome" (excessive euphoria over the belief that the Vietnam syndrome is buried) is yet another form of national denial. The evidence at this point suggests the latter interpretation more

Figure 2

closely matches our current cultural situation. In fact, the current cultural war in America reflects our national crisis of identity. This "struggle for a nation's soul"[10] is "ultimately a struggle...*over the meaning of America,* who we have been in the past, who we are now, and perhaps most important, who we, as a nation, will aspire to become in the new millennium."[11]

Three Claims

In Robert Stone's novel *Dog Soldiers,* one GI reflects on the meaning of Vietnam for American self-understanding: "Vietnam is the place where everybody finds out who they are." Another soldier responds, oblivious to the irony of his words: "What a bummer for the gooks." The first man continues as if it isn't worth debating his companion: "You can't blame us too much, we didn't know who we were until we got here. We thought we were something else."[12] This book addresses the fundamental cultural crisis articulated by that soldier — the loss of a consensus about who we are. It does so by mining the stories of one group of Americans whose lives were shattered in the 1960s and 1970s, the American combat soldiers in Vietnam. I make three claims. First, the American war in Vietnam destroyed the national consensus regarding who we are and what our mission is at home and abroad. What had been taken for granted about the meaning of America was called into question because the war contradicted the most fundamental myths that comprise the historic American identity. Some would say that Vietnam was merely about limits to American power, that its primary legacy is a more judicious calculation of the appropriate times and places to exert U.S. military muscle in the world. This view misses the deeper dimensions of the conflict. Just as the Civil War of the nineteenth century bitterly divided the nation over who we are and how we relate to one another within the bounds of the United States, so the Vietnam War raised a similar issue in regard to relationships with people of other nations. More importantly it called into question the national narrative from which this nation has historically derived its sense of identity and its role in the world.

The national narrative contains two subplots, each with internal tensions and each in tension with the other. One embodies an "alternative consciousness." These are the stories about freedom, democracy, opportunity, plenty, and justice. The other carries a "royal consciousness," namely those imperialistic pretensions that are masked by a theology of special calling wedded to an optimistic, progressive view of history.[13] This book concentrates on the "royal" plot, which I call the dominant narrative, the American Dream, "American Exceptionalism," or merely "Americanism."[14] This "royal" plot about American righteousness and invincibility unraveled in Vietnam. It is clear, however, that in the current period of transition, both subplots are under siege.

The American war in Vietnam is a major watershed in our history, but we as a nation have not fully grasped its significance or learned its lessons. We have reacted to it much as the white South reacted to defeat at the hands of the North. Rather than come to terms with the evils of slavery and the consequent racism, "recovery" was sought in "reconstruction" and a cover-up of the deep psychological and spiritual wounds brought about by slavery and defeat in the war fought to defend that institution.[15] But the demons of war cannot be dismissed so lightly. Unless they are exorcised, they act like a poison in the bloodstream of our collective unconscious, gradually leaching into every organ of national life.

Until we can explore the meaning and process the emotions that our war in Vietnam unleashed, our public energies will be dissipated in attacking symptoms rather than underlying causes of national decay and decline. George Bush painted Saddam Hussein into a diplomatic corner, making war in the Gulf inevitable in part because he wanted to put behind us the Vietnam syndrome, which Bush took to be merely public hesitancy to support large-scale U.S. military actions overseas. He failed to recognize that the Vietnam War raised fundamental questions about the nature and purpose of America itself, questions that the Gulf War did not and could not resolve.

A second claim is that the clue to understanding the effect of the war in Vietnam on American identity is not to be found in the usual places. Historians, political scientists, military strategists, diplomats, and reporters have provided us with an abundance of analyses of the causes, the strategies, and the results of this war. But it is in the stories, in the memoirs and novels, the poetry and drama, the painting and sculpture of the American combat soldiers themselves — the "grunts" — that the deepest meaning has emerged. Many of these men have spent the years since the end of the war exploring, probing, agonizing, in a life-or-death search, a search for meaning, for the meaning of America that for them was lost in the jungles and rice paddies of Vietnam. Their testimony is an exceptionally powerful form of narrative theology probing the experience of exile, alienation, darkness, and healing. Only gradually and fitfully is new meaning emerging from this secular arena of American story theology.[16]

Much has been written about the great diversity of combat experiences. "Vietnam was many things. It varied year by year, place by place, unit by unit."[17] Anyone who knows a number of vets or interviews a cross section of them or peruses the great variety of literature on this war will agree that from the standpoint of the participants there were in fact many wars. However, there are certain common denominators that appear in most of these war stories. The similarity of perspective that informs much of the literature is surprising, given the diversity of combat experiences. The vast majority of memoirs, autobiographies, and action stories fit neatly into the classic genre of American male adventure on the frontier. Even the very moving tales of suffering and indomitable courage by prisoners of war like Vice Admiral James Bond Stockdale stay within rather conventional boundaries of interpretation.[18]

However, an alternate version of the Vietnam experience exists in oral and written narrative and on film. A careful study of some of the best literature, supplemented by oral interviews with combat vets, yields a core of similar interpretations that contradict the conventional stories. Their depth and power convey an honesty, an integrity, and an authenticity that call into question the validity of our traditional national self-understanding. In these narratives the good guys don't always win; in fact the very dichotomy "good guys/bad guys," which animates so much of our national myth, is destroyed. This core of similar but alternative interpretations can be described by two major metaphors: descent into the heart of darkness and the journey through the dark night of the soul. Each one of

these metaphors receives chapter-length treatment in the
pages that follow.

In Vietnam when a squad of soldiers moved out from its
firebase to explore the jungle, one man was designated to
take the lead, to "walk point." He was not an advance scout
sent to spy and report back. He was an integral part of the
fighting unit, its eyes and ears, placed in the most vulnerable position of leading his unit into battle. "Walking point"
meant first exposure to land mines, booby traps, sniper
fire, and ambush. Such men gained a sixth sense for danger and sent back warning signals to the rest of the unit.
Analogously, combat soldiers in the war in Vietnam have
"walked point" for America, exploring uncharted territory
in our unfolding national story. They are our contemporary pilgrims, the modern-day descendants of our pioneer
forebears. Because they bear in their bodies and souls the
wounds of that perilous journey taken on our behalf and
because their experience uncovers the folly of the journey itself, I believe that in a certain sense they have taken
on a role for America similar to that of the suffering ser-
vant described in Isaiah 53. The Christian application of
this passage to Jesus of Nazareth has so overshadowed our
understanding of this text that it is difficult — and perhaps for some offensive — to apply this passage to other
historical figures. Nonetheless, if we stick to the literal
sense of the text, its application to Vietnam vets is hard to
deny:

> He was despised and rejected by others;
> a man of suffering and acquainted with infirmity;
> and as one from whom others hide their faces
> he was despised, and we held him of no account.
> Surely he has borne our infirmities and carried our
>   diseases;
> yet we accounted him stricken, struck down by God
>   and afflicted.
> But he was wounded for our transgressions, crushed
>   for our iniquities;

upon him was the punishment that made us whole,
and by his bruises we are healed. (Isaiah 53:3–5)

Let there be no misunderstanding. I am not claiming
that American vets are any more virtuous than the rest
of us. The claim is simply this: willingly or unwillingly,
they paid the price of our national hubris, a hubris embedded in our narratives of national identity. By attending
to their stories — selectively to be sure — we may discover the idolatrous character of our collective story. By
embracing their wisdom, revealed in darkness and struggle, we may discover how to alter our national purpose.
Henri Nouwen has written, "Who can take away suffering without entering into it?"[19] Only the wounded, says
Nouwen, can be healers. I make no claim, however, that
vets are *automatically* "wounded healers."

A visit to "The Wall" in Washington (the Vietnam Veterans Memorial) provides the occasion for a dramatic
reenactment of the war. The Wall is shaped like an enormous V carved into the Mall. The entrance leads the
visitor down one side of the V into the very bowels of the
earth, as it were. The reflecting black marble containing
name after name after name — over fifty-eight thousand —
draws the visitor into itself, revealing the magnitude of
evil, tragedy, loss. Some visitors start down one side, then
turn around and leave before they experience the abyss.
So also with vets and with us as a nation. Even the most
articulate, who describe in agonizing detail the darkness
they have entered, can become healers only by moving
through the abyss and up the other side of the V. This
requires the transvaluation of aspects of our national narrative, so that the dark side of our national history can be
confessed rather than glorified. Vets suffering from post–
traumatic stress disorder (PTSD) have discovered the truth
of Nouwen's rhetorical question. As long as they try to
avoid or deny the evil of their experiences — both those
"in country" (Vietnam), and those "back in the world" (the
United States) — their suffering spreads like a malignancy.

Only when they begin the journey back into the night does a ray of light shine through.

At an intuitive level many vets recognize the vicarious nature of the suffering they still experience. Our national attempt to ignore their experience and revise the Vietnam story by scapegoating the press, the military, the government, the vets themselves, or the antiwar movement merely adds to their sense of betrayal. Indeed, it compounds their suffering by giving them the impression that their sacrifice was in vain. I contend that many of these vets are prophets. As recipients of a new self-knowledge, they carry within their bodies and souls a revelatory wisdom that is essential for the reconstruction of a postwar American national identity. The journey beyond our contemporary cultural wars passes inexorably through the fires of their Vietnam experience. The American war in Vietnam was a logical product of our historic "errand into the wilderness." Until we as a nation have understood the vets' wilderness experience we will not be able to come to terms with the dark side of our inherited national identity. If we do risk embarking on this corporate journey for which certain vets are "walking point," we may find a way out of our current cultural war into a new and healthier national identity and corporate purpose.

A final claim is that mainline religious bodies have an essential role to play in forging a new American identity. The theology that American soldiers took with them to Vietnam was woefully inadequate for making sense out of that experience. This was due partly to their youthfulness — the median age of American combat soldiers in Vietnam was 19.6 years, as opposed to over 25 years in World War II. Nonetheless, the apparently innocuous mixture of Americanism and Christianity that they had imbibed from childhood in home, school, and church provided little assistance for interpreting wartime experiences. In fact, it proved idolatrous and lethal. In some ways analogous to the national theology of the state church in Nazi Germany that provided no room for opposition to

Hitler, the civil religion of our GIs and many of their chaplains proved powerless to interpret their experience of evil; powerless to resist the moral corrosion of a political and military command structure mired in self-deception; and powerless to save them from despair and often suicide. Over fifty-eight thousand U.S. troops were killed in Vietnam. It is estimated that between sixty thousand and one hundred thousand have committed suicide since returning from the war.

By the time the Vietnam War ended, most mainline denominations had turned against the war and those who fought it. John Fergueson, who participated in torture and assassination as part of the Special Forces Phoenix program, went through a dark night of the soul on his way toward ministry as an Episcopal priest. He tells of his experience in the mid 1970s at a spiritual retreat for clergy: "We were in group prayer, people were confessing their sins; friends sitting nearby would touch them and the leaders would utter some words of forgiveness and encouragement. I was overcome with emotion and prayed, 'Thank you God for forgiving me about Vietnam.' Everyone was stunned. A deadly silence followed. No one touched me; some got up and walked out. Blasphemy! I didn't belong; I wasn't worthy of forgiveness."[20]

That experience is not unique. Many mainline pastors now recognize their complicity in the rejection of Vietnam vets and in the self-righteous tone of the antiwar movement within the churches. Even those who were opposed to Desert Storm were careful to voice their support for the soldiers who fought in the Persian Gulf. However, Vietnam vets have by and large left the churches; those who remain feel uncomfortable there. The problem lies not in any stigma — we've moved beyond that now — nor in lack of pastoral care. Rather, the main obstacle is theological, the nature of the "gospel" that is heard and practiced in churches. Those who have descended into the abyss are offended by the myths of American innocence and virtue and a religion thoroughly immersed in optimism and material pursuit. They hunger for a God who hears the cries of those who have descended into hell and feel abandoned or betrayed. They thirst for a gospel that can, in Auden's words, "make a vineyard of the curse." They long for a church — and a society — that listens to their agony and attends to the wisdom revealed through them. This book provides an interpretive guide into the most profound experiences of these veterans, so that by learning from them, religious communities and others can contribute more creatively to the search for a new national identity and purpose.

Chapter 1 lays out the theoretical framework for interpreting both the war experience of veterans and the collective loss of national purpose that followed the war. It moves away from the war itself to a discussion of story, myth, narrative, and other elements of personal and corporate identity, demonstrating how identity is created, maintained, and destroyed. The tone of chapter 1 is more abstract than that of the other chapters. For this reason, the reader may wish to jump ahead to chapters 2 through 7 before returning to chapter 1 for a systematic presentation on the narrative character of personal and national identity.

Chapter One

Identity

The Loss of a Dream

Figure 3

Figure 3 appeared in the *San Francisco Sunday Examiner and Chronicle* in July 1992.[1] Two weeks later the front page of the same newspaper carried a story by Lynn Ludlow entitled "Doors Foreclosing on American Dream," which noted that in San Francisco the number of families losing their homes to foreclosures had jumped from 7.3 per month in

1988 to 41 per month in 1992. Being expelled from one's place in the American Dream can spell more than a temporary threat to one's identity; it sometimes leads to suicide. "Life's final sound for a high-flying Marin County businessman," wrote Ludlow, "was the purr of his Mercedes as it filled the garage with carbon monoxide. Although his home was forfeit to the crash of his finances, friends said he couldn't bring himself to say a word to his unsuspecting wife and children."[2]

In the midst of the daily bombardment we call "information overload," it would be easy to overlook the significance of this tiny news bite. We could dismiss it as a story about the kind of temporary economic phenomena that always accompany the nadir of recessions, an inexorable product of the inevitable business cycle. The cartoon, however, spurs us to look deeper, to understand the American Dream as more than a commitment to the economic premise that "more is better." Just as the corporate identity of former Soviet citizens has been fundamentally altered by the demise of the Soviet Union, so the American Dream is a metaphor for a common national identity that is now in question. Economic decline is merely one manifestation of the deeper cultural crisis, the uncertainty about who we are as a people and where we are going as a nation. For many American vets the American Dream died long ago in the forests and rice paddies of Vietnam.

To understand the nature of this loss, it is necessary to explore a framework for understanding personal and corporate identity and the processes by which identity is maintained and changed. This framework will provide clues and categories for understanding how the experiences of certain Vietnam vets shattered their personal identities and simultaneously undermined their inherited sense of national identity. Such an understanding is essential for grasping the representative role these vets play for all Americans in the current national search for a revised common identity.

The widespread contemporary interest in the study of

narrative has led some to regard identity and narrative as almost synonymous. Narratives do more than describe the past; they explain the present and shape the future. This applies at both the personal and the social level. One specialist in narrative theology remarks, "A community is a group of people who have come to share a common past, who understand events in the past to be of decisive importance for interpreting the present, who anticipate the future by means of a shared hope, and who express their identity by means of a common narrative. . . . The community's common narrative is the glue that binds its members together."[3]

Among the scholars who specialize in the literature of the American war in Vietnam it is axiomatic that continuities and changes in both personal and national identity are to be discerned primarily through a study of narrative. John Hellmann's *American Myth and the Legacy of Vietnam*[4] is perhaps the most explicit in this regard, but the analytical/critical works of Philip Beidler, Tobey C. Herzog, Philip K. Jason, Bill Mahedy, Philip Melling, Thomas Myers, John Clark Pratt, William Searle, and others whose writings are drawn upon in later chapters all reflect this assumption. So also the GIs who write memoirs and novels about the war.

However, identity is more than narrative alone. It also includes elements of commitment, sacralization, and ritual.[5] In this chapter each of these four elements will be examined formally, then illustrated briefly by reference to the American experience in Vietnam. The chapters that follow will draw upon and illustrate these theoretical concepts. The first task is to offer a definition of identity that incorporates these four elements.

A Definition of Identity

Who are you? The simplest of questions, yet also one of the most profound. Every time we make a phone call or meet a new person we identify ourselves and ask the other person to do the same. After an exchange of names we deepen the search: "Where do you live?" "What do you do?" "Where are you from?" As the other person responds we listen not only for the answers to our explicit questions but also for answers to those unexpressed questions we raise only in our minds: "Is this accent Boston Irish or New York Jewish?" "Is she Nigerian or Jamaican?" "Are these clothes from Saks Fifth Avenue or L. L. Bean?" "Labor or management?" "Gay or straight?" "On my right, politically, or on my left?" These simple questions provide clues to the components that comprise one level of identity. We discover who people are by situating them in the world, by locating their place, the groups to which they belong, the work they do, their status, the roles they play, their values and allegiances, and their personal styles and tastes. And our interaction with them begins with an intuitive assessment of our similarities and differences and how our identities overlap or diverge.

Social psychologists are prone to regard identity as "the conglomeration of roles which are the product of social expectations and personal response."[6] According to this view, to know people it is enough to understand the roles they play and the personal style used in playing these roles. There is much to be said for this definition, especially in an economy where success is determined largely by how one fares in the market.[7] In the end, however, this definition of identity is inadequate. While it may account for the plurality of "selves" exhibited by a person's diverse behavior, it does not account for the unity and continuity that are expressed through that person's multiple "selves." In addition, it appears rather mechanical and one-way, ignoring the nuanced interaction between person and society. It begs the question because it does nothing to explain why we willingly select certain roles and the social expectations that accompany those roles. It is too other-directed, leaving aside the inner coherence and integrity of personhood. Even the pressure of society itself tends to emphasize such inner coherence: society demands not merely that we *act* good but that we *be* good. In other words, in condemning hypocrisy society expects that the motivation for fulfilling role expectations will come not merely from social pressure but also from inner conviction.

In *Death of a Salesman*, Arthur Miller provides a tragic portrait of a man who is nothing more than a conglomeration of the roles he plays, especially his economic role. Miller tells us that as a salesman Willy Loman is the archetypal person whom a market economy produces. He even sells himself. After his death the most fitting epitaph for his life is: "Poor Willy. He never knew who he was."

The inner coherence and integrity of personhood are captured best by regarding personal identity as layered, involving a surface and a depth or core.[8] At the surface lie our physical characteristics, the roles we play, our opinions, and much of our nonconsequential behavior. At the core of our selfhood — the metaphorical level — lie those narratives that are the bearers of the beliefs, values, and goals providing unity and continuity to the self. Erik Erikson points to this deeper level when he describes identity as "a persistent sameness within oneself (self-sameness) and a persistent sharing of some kind of essential character with others."[9] This definition takes into account the self-determination of the person as well as the formative influences emanating from society.

This inner coherence involves both a conscious and an unconscious striving for persistent sameness, as well as an effort to *deepen* personal character, to become more like the image of who we are in our essential being. Christian theology has traditionally examined the striving for greater realization of our authentic being under the rubric of sanctification. "Be who you are!" is more than a parental nudge toward obedient behavior. This *ought* appears deeply embedded within the *is* of our being, an impulse urging us, for good or ill, toward the realization of our most cherished values and goals.

Basic military training is designed to do more than teach a person how to play the role of a soldier. Boot camp seeks to transform the essential being of a civilian into that of a soldier who learns not only to kill but to gain a sense of accomplishment — of self-fulfillment — in performing those skills that result in killing. For many American soldiers in Vietnam, where success was defined by the body count, this actualization of their new identity involved a gradual descent into a "heart of darkness." In the darkness their identity as soldiers, as Americans, and even as human beings began to disintegrate.

We can return now to the exploration of the meaning of identity. The "persistent sameness" and "essential character" referred to above are explained better by the core narratives (and the beliefs, values, and goals embedded in those narratives) that a person embraces than by the roles they play. It is these core elements that structure identity and give subordinate elements their relative place in the hierarchy of a person's life. This is in line with Paul Tillich's definition of religion as ultimate concern and with H. Richard Niebuhr's view that "the necessity of believing in a god is given with the life of selves."[10]

Erikson's emphasis on the "persistent sharing of some kind of essential character with others" points to the social dimension of identity and the fact that identity is formed through social discourse. We may play various roles with varying degrees of enthusiasm, but the more solidarity we feel with a particular social group the deeper our internalization of that group's beliefs, values, and goals. A major factor in distinguishing types of soldiers/veterans and their varying reactions to their wartime experiences is the degree to which they willingly and eagerly embraced the myths of America, the ideals of the military, and the specific goals of U.S. policy before landing in Vietnam.

The emphasis on persistence, continuity, and sameness should not blind us to the dynamic dimensions of identity. At every level of identity — person, group, and society — there is a dialectic between the forces for stability and the forces for change. A simplified representation of these forces appears in figure 4.[11] The basic need for

Figure 4

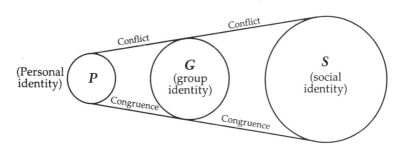

order and security at each level exerts pressure toward a convergence and congruence of beliefs, values, ideals, goals, role expectations, and so on within each level and between levels. At the same time there exists a contrary set of pressures toward divergence and change. The two actually complement each other. Too much convergence leads to excessive stability and rigidity, even totalitarianism; too much conflict and change leads to disorder and chaos. Frequently changes at one level that strengthen identity at that level produce changes that weaken identity at other levels. For example, the various recipes for self-realization in American culture may strengthen personal identity by weakening family life and commitment to society. In China, on the other hand, Maoist ideology attacked filial piety, thus weakening the identity of the family while simultaneously strengthening national identity and altering the historic Confucian understanding of the structure of human community.

The interdependence of these three levels of identity is evident in Vietnam War narratives. As a rule, vets whose families and peer groups also turned against the war and the national narrative behind it have found it less difficult to forge a new postwar identity than those without such familial and peer-group support. The latter are more likely to engage in various forms of scapegoating, while being torn between their own disillusionment with the national story and the uncritical embrace of that story by their family and peer groups.

Having considered various dimensions of identity, a fuller definition can now be offered. The clue comes from the comment above that identity is forged in conversation. In this ongoing conversation one maintains a simultaneous running dialogue with many partners: the tradition or traditions (whatever they may be), the groups to which one belongs, the larger society of which one is a part, and the god or gods (highest values or ultimate concerns) one worships. Thus identity involves a three-dimensional conversation. It consists of length (the traditions in which one is rooted), breadth (the relationships one has with other persons and groups in society), and depth (the quality of self-reflection a person brings to his or her traditions, relationships, and experiences).[12] Like a choir director who adds her or his own voice to the music, a person has the freedom and the necessity to select which partner speaks when and to blend the voices of the various conversation partners into a coherent story, at times raising the volume of some voices and lowering the volume of others. Personal identity may be defined, then, as the narrative a person enacts (lives out of and into). This story is reinforced — and frequently sacralized — by rituals that engender commitment.

Social identity at the small-group level is similar to collective identity at the national level. It also consists of narrative interpretations of reality that are enacted, reinforced, and often sacralized by commitment-engendering rituals. For purely analytical purposes these four dimensions of identity — narrative, commitment, sacralization, ritual — can be separated, although in reality they are always simultaneously present and in constant, overlapping interaction.

Narrative

Human beings possess an innate need and instinct for meaning. Order and security at the personal as well as the social level require a coherent interpretation of reality that makes sense of experience and provides structure for human existence. Kurt Vonnegut satirized this fundamental human imperative in his novel *Cat's Cradle*. At the moment of his creation, Adam blinks and questions God: " 'What is the purpose of all this?' 'Everything must have a purpose?' asked God. 'Certainly,' said Adam. 'Then I leave it to you to think of one for all this,' said God."[13] Then God went away.

This assumption of a basic human drive to eliminate all forms of meaninglessness undergirded the entire work of the classical sociologist Max Weber. Further, the assumption is key in the work of Viktor Frankl, the father of logotherapy who developed the "Third Viennese School of Psychotherapy" as an alternative to the schools founded by Sigmund Freud and Alfred Adler. Freud stressed the *pleasure principle* and Adler the *will to power*, but to Frankl "the striving to find a meaning . . . is the primary motivational force" in human life.[14]

A. J. Ungersma, a student of Frankl's, understands these three drives developmentally. During childhood the pleasure principle dominates; in adolescence the power principle overshadows everything else; in adulthood the will to meaning takes precedence.[15] Ungersma's insight sheds light on the experiences of veterans. Most were between adolescence and adulthood when they went to Vietnam, seeking an identity. What better place than a war to test one's mettle, become a man, assert one's will to power? The failure of the will to power in Vietnam may account for the fact that many vets still suffer from unresolved adolescent issues, especially those related to identity. The inability to resolve this developmental crisis may explain the longevity of post–traumatic stress disorder (PTSD) and why some vets are not yet able to move to the next developmental stage, which is to reconstruct a meaningful worldview.

Sometimes writing about their war experiences becomes a part of the therapeutic process of recovery from PTSD. Robert Mason's *Chickenhawk*[16] is an example. His poignant description of the skills required to maneuver a damaged helicopter down into and then out of a jungle landing zone amid enemy fire is a classic testimony to the vitality of the drive to survive, the need to overcome adversity, the will to power. This theme surfaces again and again in the Vietnam literature. The best of the literature, however, goes beyond that and can be understood as an expression of the will to meaning, as a search for interpretive categories for sense-making after all meaning had been shattered in Vietnam.

If the will to meaning is a basic human drive, *narrative* is the form that meaning takes. Our construction of a worldview, our ordering of reality that some sociologists call the "nomizing" process,[17] takes narrative form. Our structured narratives organize the endless succession of social events into a meaningful pattern with temporal and causal sequences that have affective as well as intellectual dimensions. Thus, narratives not only structure our consciousness along certain lines; they also encourage specific attitudes and suggest specific forms of behavior. Explicitly and implicitly, stories provide simultaneous explanations, feelings, and ethical imperatives. They explain how things are, how we should feel about them, and what we should do as a result of them. One problem that therapists face at PTSD units of VA (Veterans Administration) hospitals derives from the secular character of healing in government agencies. By steering clear of the most fundamental religious narratives that give meaning to the vets' experience of darkness, therapists who are not also chaplains often ignore the way emotions are socially constructed by narratives and how at the deepest levels of healing therapy depends upon religious metaphors and stories.

In recent years narrative has gained increasing attention

from scholars in many disciplines. It is now recognized that human existence itself is narrative in character[18] and that persons and communities "dream in narrative, daydream in narrative, remember, anticipate, hope, despair, believe, doubt, plan, revise, criticize, construct, gossip, learn, hate and love by narrative."[19] Narrative is the glue that holds life together both at the personal and at the societal level.

At first scholars regarded narrative theology as a fad, the product of "soft" thinking that was not up to the rigors of "higher" forms of abstract rationality. Today there is a growing recognition by philosophers and scientists alike both of the limits of rationality and of the narrative character of rationality.[20] We now recognize that the Enlightenment, which enthroned reason, debunked myth, and set science in opposition to art, is itself a complex web of myths; that the Enlightenment worldview is itself "a story that tells us we have outgrown stories."[21] Thus, the choice is not between myth and rationality, as Rudolf Bultmann would have it in his project of demythologization. The choice is between more viable and less viable myths, between narratives that are validated or invalidated by experience. As we shall see later on, the primary identity-forming narratives of the American GIs who served in Vietnam provided an inadequate framework for interpreting their experience. For them, the American narrative itself died in Vietnam. As a result, the vets' search for healing first takes the form of angry narrative deconstruction, and then a life-or-death struggle for narrative reconstruction begins.

If worldviews are narrative in form, what are the *forms of narrative?* Thus far we have been using the terms "story," "myth," and "narrative" as if they were almost synonymous, and many writers employ these words interchangeably. This usage may be confusing, however, because "story" and "myth" are often synonyms for fable and falsehood. Thus, a more careful distinction among the various forms of narrative is necessary.

John Dominic Crossan's widely accepted typology of narrative genres serves our purposes well. For Crossan, narrative takes five fundamental forms, each with a different function: "Story establishes world in *myth*, defends such established world in *apologue*, discusses and describes world in *action*, attacks world in *satire*, and subverts world in *parable*."[22] Some dispute the sharp distinction Crossan draws between the mythic and the parabolic narrative, maintaining that narrative often performs mythoparabolic functions simultaneously.[23]

Although most of the memoirs and novels of the American war in Vietnam include elements of three or even four of these genres, usually one genre predominates. In fact the identification of the dominant genre is usually a clue to the writer's moral assessment of the war, the depth of the identity crisis produced by the war, and the character of the sense-making responsibilities left in its wake. For example, Ron Kovic's memoir, *Born on the Fourth of July* (and the film based on it), carries both mythic and satiric elements because it reinforces the hero myth of the Lone Ranger (Kovic) even while attacking the establishment (Nixon's 1972 Republican Convention). Robert Mason's *Chickenhawk* stays primarily at the descriptive level of action. Jack Fuller's *Fragments* and the works of Philip Caputo, Larry Heinemann, and Gustav Hasford (referred to later) fall primarily into the categories of satire and parable.

Let us keep these narrative genres in mind as we examine the contributions that commitment and sacralization make to identity. Just as the different genres provide clues to a writer's moral assessment of the war, so the type of narrative a person lives by reveals the character of her or his selfhood.

Commitment and Sacralization

Knowledge of individuals' stories or societies' narratives is an insufficient guide to understanding their identity. By itself, narrative provides only a clue to a person's or a society's general worldview and system of meaning. It does not tell us how firmly attached each is to that narrative or how likely each is to act in accordance with it. For this we must also know the degree of commitment to the narrative and the degree to which that story or narrative has been sacralized.

Commitment refers to the degree of a person's emotional attachment to a particular focus of identity. These foci can be as vague as salvation or Nirvana in the world religions or as specific as the pragmatic goals of fame and fortune. One study of identity in the United States in the late 1960s examined a plethora of identity foci including cults, recreation, health, heroes and celebrities, and social crusades.[24] Today we might add professional sports to this list, as well as psychotherapeutic cults of self-fulfillment. Each of these foci may function as a *summum bonum* (supreme good), providing a narrative with beliefs, values, and goals for centering and integrating personal and social life.

If a high degree of devotion, trust, faith, surrender, and absolute dependence — synonyms for commitment — can be applied to these foci, then they function as gods, providing integration, motivation, and direction to the person or group. By calling attention to the narrative dimension of identity, the specific focus of emotional attachment is placed in a larger context with a history and a destiny. Thus, following our earlier discussion, we can describe commitment as emotional attachment to a specific narrative.

Max Weber's insight into the way in which the Protestant ethic of "inner-worldly asceticism" served to foster the entrepreneurial spirit of European capitalism illustrates the connection between narrative and commitment. Weber understood commitment to be both cognitive and affective; it involves attachment both to intellectual explanations — the theology, or, in our terminology, the narrative — and to practical action in the world on the basis of that theology.

Commitment fulfills several functions for the person and for the society. In addition to its role in personal and social integration, which we have already noted, commitment also yields consistency of behavior by shaping the ethical choices we make and the actions we take. What we care about we attend to, so that commitment molds our thought patterns and the way we process data, interpret our experience, and make sense of the world. This in turn produces reliability and predictability. No wonder the military prefers volunteers to draftees and places so much stress on basic training. Young people are recruited in late adolescence when, developmentally, they are engaged in forming an adult identity. The primary goal of boot camp is to erase their youthful civilian identity and replace it with a highly motivated, gung ho martial identity. In being so changed new recruits become responsible and predictable within the military structure. As with any bureaucracy, only those who show high commitment as well as advanced skills are promoted in rank.

One reason hypocrisy is universally condemned by all societies is that it masks actual commitments, thus reducing reliability and predictability.[25] By undermining trust, hypocrisy weakens social solidarity; in its place, doubt and cynicism emerge. In the next five chapters we will examine the corrosive legacy of official military and political hypocrisy and self-deception stemming from the war in Vietnam. As the gap between the ideological rationale and the stated goals of the war, on the one hand, and the actual implementation of strategy, on the other, became clearer to the troops, their anger and cynicism grew. So did their unwillingness to pursue what they came to regard as an illegitimate war. A major component of PTSD is the alienation soldiers experienced upon their return to the United States when they discovered not only that they were victims of hypocrisy but also that the sacrifices they had made for their country were condemned rather than honored.

Commitment usually involves some form of sacrifice because attachment to a particular focus of identity (a specific narrative with its attendant values) requires the relegation of other values to secondary or tertiary importance. Sacrifice thereby reinforces identity by clarifying priorities. By ranking some goals as more important than others, commitment to those selected is strengthened. If the sacrifice is extreme — for example, a severe wound — it may serve almost like a photographic "fixer" solution, establishing an identity and enhancing commitment to the narrative that expresses that identity.

However, if the larger narrative itself is called into question, sacrifice on its behalf may lead to disillusionment and alienation. This irony helps explain the multifaceted ambivalence of Vietnam veterans. Although they are sharply critical of the American military and government, their identity has been shaped by their war experience and the sacrifices made on behalf of their country. Many joined the antiwar movement upon their return to the United States but soon felt victimized by the doves as well. The flag-burning and America-bashing of the antiwar movement mocked the good-faith sacrifices they had made for their country, so that in the end they felt abandoned and betrayed by all sectors of American society.

Commitment is a step in the direction of its close cousin, sacralization. Sacralization is the process whereby the focus of identity — the particular story, its narrative content, and the worldview it carries — develops a taken-for-granted quality, an unquestioned givenness. By enveloping a system of meaning in sentiments of awe and untouchableness, sacralization protects a person from meaninglessness and anomie. Like immunization at the biological level, sacralization at the symbolic level provides closure and protection from the relativism implicit in competing views of reality.[26]

A sacralized system of meaning provides a strong defense against alternative interpretations of reality, but when a sacred narrative is shattered by experience, a traumatic identity crisis is produced. The person either "converts" to an alternative narrative, if one is readily available, or wanders erratically in a wilderness without meaning. The latter is the experience of many vets. World War II vindicated the traditional narrative of American messianism; the cold war provided a clear and simple explanation of the forces of good and evil in the world; Kennedy's New Frontier evoked high-minded visions of national purpose. These, together with the total obedience induced by military training, produced a tightly held, highly sacralized worldview. Kovic's *Born on the Fourth of July* illustrates this sacralization as well as any Vietnam War narrative.

When the American war in Vietnam was called into question by the antiwar movement, supporters responded as if an ancient taboo had been broken, an indication of the sacralized character of war in the American narrative. The administration and the military brass correctly perceived this movement as an attack on the American narrative, a threat to troop morale, and a restriction on their ability to wage war in Indochina. Likewise, when massive disillusionment set in among the American troops after the Vietcong's Tet Offensive in 1968, the troops' commitment to the war effort turned into widespread cynicism toward their officers, toward "lifers" (career soldiers), toward the Pentagon, and toward the U.S. government in general. Their god (sacred narrative) had failed. Thus, the goals of the troops and the goals of the military diverged until they were in opposition to one another: the military counted corpses, but the troops counted days. For the GIs, personal survival and escape back to "the world" (the United States) at the end of their 365-day tour of duty in Vietnam replaced the goals of the national narrative.

Ritual

If identity is the narrative to which we are committed, the narrative out of which and into which we live, ritual is the means by which the world depicted in the narrative is established, reinforced, and changed. Rituals are the ceremonies society provides for participating in communal narratives. They are simultaneously historical and hermeneutical: they enact the stories of the past while at the same time supporting a particular interpretation of that past. In so doing they help shape a particular future. "Societies rest upon shared understandings of world and reality that are constituted *ritually* through *shared performance*" of communal narrative.[27]

When understandings of world and reality are not shared, ritual performance is either ambivalent or oppressive for some of the participants. The controversy surrounding the Columbus quincentennial rituals in the San Francisco Bay Area illustrates this point. During the preceding year heated debate took place over the meaning of our national history and the way it is remembered in ritual ceremonies. Earlier, San Francisco had won the national competition to host the official 1992 Columbus Day celebration in the United States. Recently built replicas of Columbus's ships were scheduled to sail into San Francisco Bay to launch the ceremonies. Then Resistance 500, a coalition of Native Americans and others, began protesting the proposed festival. The chair of the quincentennial committee resigned early on; the visit of the three ships was canceled; and what was slated to be a unifying, triumphal festival commemorating our common national heritage was transformed into a multifaceted protest/celebration underscoring the conflicting narratives of national identity. When October 12, 1992, finally arrived, some in San Francisco engaged in a ritual reenactment of the daring and triumphant "discovery" of America, replete with the regal glory of the Spanish queen Isabella and friendly "Indians." At the same time, across the bay in Berkeley, others celebrated Indigenous Peoples' Day and ritually mourned the Columbus event and the subsequent "five hundred years of pillage and genocide."

Among the many anthropologists who have studied the functions of rituals, Arnold Van Gennep and Victor

Turner have produced works that are particularly relevant to a study of the American war in Vietnam.[28] Van Gennep coined the phrase "rites of passage" to describe rituals in which a person moves from one status or condition in society to another.[29] These include common life-cycle rituals (for example, ceremonies at birth and death, naming ceremonies, baptism, initiation or puberty rites, graduation, marriage, retirement) as well as changes in relationship, such as the move from outsider to insider, from enemy to friend, and so forth. Van Gennep recognized that the movement that takes place in a person's life when one status is given up and another is acquired has three distinct stages. This movement can be likened to the physical displacement that takes place when a person moves from one dwelling to another. To leave "home" (a particular status) is to cross the threshold of one's former dwelling. For a time one is in limbo, status-free. Then another threshold is crossed as one enters the new "home" (status). Thus, taking the Latin word for threshold, *limen,* Van Gennep discerned three types of rituals: the *preliminal* (rites that separate persons or groups from a former status or condition); the *liminal* (rites that conduct them "through a nothingness, a temporary loss of identity in a time that [is] no time and a place that [is] nowhere");[30] and the *postliminal* (rites that reincorporate them into society but in a new status or position). The same schema may be applied to social events, even large-scale changes in society such as the end of the cold war and the reincorporation of the nations of Eastern Europe and the former Soviet Union into the world market economy.

Van Gennep's *Rites of Passage* was first published in 1908. Since then many anthropologists have used his framework to study social processes, but perhaps the most nuanced work on rituals has been done by a contemporary anthropologist, Victor Turner. He has refined Van Gennep's thought, placing particular emphasis on the liminal character of all rituals.

The liminal stage is fraught with danger and awe because normal rules and expectations are in abeyance. Among the Ndembu people in Africa, whom Turner studied, liminality may be likened "to death, to being in the womb, to invisibility, to darkness, to bisexuality, to the wilderness, and to an eclipse of the sun or moon."[31] For other cultures, whatever situations evoke fear and trembling are liminal.

This framework is particularly useful for analyzing the transitions from civilian to soldier and back again to civilian. In fact, whether in conversation or in writing most veterans of every war automatically describe their experiences as rites of passage filled with liminal periods. Each stage — the arrival of the draft notice, induction, boot camp, arrival at the site of combat, the first engagement with the enemy, the first encounter with death, the gradual descent into darkness, and finally the journey back home, reunion with one's family, discharge from the military, the onset of PTSD, and the struggle for healing — can be understood better by examining it in the context of the larger framework first articulated by Van Gennep and then developed by Turner.

Rituals provide us with three "social gifts":[32] (1) they establish, maintain, and restore *order* in society; (2) they create and sustain *community* by bringing about a spirit of unity and common affection; and (3) they *transform* and redirect society. These anthropological claims for ritual echo Crossan's claims for different types of narrative. This is no accident, for if myth creates world, action explores world, and parable subverts world,[33] and if ritual is enacted story, then we should expect that different types of ritual will serve different functions, depending upon the type of story that is enacted in each.

At times a ritual may combine different types of stories, so that some rituals are mythoparabolic, sustaining a particular worldview while at the same time criticizing and undermining it. Most of the October 12, 1992, ceremonies either supported the Columbus myth and a positive evaluation of the past five hundred years or attacked that myth with a negative commentary on those five centuries. However, in certain worship services an attempt was made to combine the mythic and the parabolic, the ordering and the disordering, by recognizing the ambiguity of our religious and national heritage. Each of these functions or social gifts will be examined separately.

1. *Order:* The first function of ritual is to establish order by providing an explanation of the way a people understands the world. "Through ritualization we make routine a certain way of seeing, hearing, touching, and otherwise perceiving the environment."[34] The ancient Hebrews celebrated their founding narrative of ethnic identity annually in the ritual of the harvest of the firstfruits. After the priest placed the basket of firstfruits before the altar of the Lord, the worshiper was instructed to recite a five-part summary of the sacred Hebrew saga of nomadic wandering, sojourning in Egypt, oppression in Egypt, deliverance from oppression, and the gift of a land flowing with milk and honey. An entire worldview is included in this short historical narrative, a view that includes a doctrine of God (the one who hears human cries and intervenes to deliver and sustain) and a doctrine of human nature (steward of this gracious God). By repeating this ritual annually, national unity was rehearsed and reinforced.

Such dramatic reenactment of the existing order of things happens regularly in every society. Robert Grimes provides a detailed analysis of the public rituals that support the current social order and interethnic relationships among Indian, Hispanic, and Anglo residents in Santa Fe, New Mexico.[35] The first ritual involves a public procession of La Conquistadora, a statue of the Virgin Mary, led by the Roman Catholic bishop. It takes place in early summer and reinforces Catholic power and Hispanic culture. The Spanish had been expelled by a Pueblo uprising in 1680 during which four hundred Spaniards were killed. In 1692, according to the story, Don Diego De Vargas came to Santa Fe and pleaded with the Indians to return to Spanish culture and religion. Unarmed and accompanied only by La Conquistadora, he entered the city; an accommodation was reached without any bloodshed.

In late summer a pageant reenacts this 1692 peaceful "reconquest" of New Mexico by De Vargas. What is omitted, however, is any mention of the fact that in 1693 De Vargas returned with a large military force and demanded total surrender. When the Indians refused and fighting broke out, a number of Indians were killed. Others were taken as indentured slaves by De Vargas's troops. In the contemporary pageant, a revisionist narrative is enacted, asserting that present-day interethnic relationships are derived from an original racial harmony. "The pageant obviously focuses on 1692 alone in order to emphasize the historical grounds for harmonious Hispano-Indian relations. In fact, the moral of the pageant is that the contemporary 'tricultural existence' is a direct result of De Vargas' peaceful and imaginative tactics. The pageant implies that De Vargas knew exactly what his deeds promised for future generations."[36] Independence Day, Thanksgiving, Memorial Day, and Veterans Day function in analogous ways for American society as a whole.

In like manner, ritual restores order when it has been disrupted. A ritualized "social drama" unfolds in four stages. A *breach* occurs; a *crisis* ensues; some measure of *redress* is taken; and finally some form of *resolution* takes place.[37] The military judicial system provides a typical example of this four-stage social drama. A soldier disobeys orders; an officer presses charges; a court-martial is conducted; the soldier is found innocent or guilty, followed by the dismissal of charges or some form of punishment. At each stage of the process order is reinforced by the implicit assumption of the legitimacy of the code of behavior that has been breached, as well as by the implicit legitimacy granted to the judicial system itself. If the legitimacy of the military judicial system is called into question (as indeed it was in the latter years of the war in Vietnam), the underlying narrative that explains and justifies the military itself also comes under attack.

In early 1971 the Vietnam Veterans Against the War (VVAW) organized a three-day Winter Soldier Investigation in response to the trial of Lieutenant William Calley. Its purpose was to demonstrate by public testimony from GIs who had served in Vietnam that "My Lai was not an isolated incident" but "only a minor step beyond the standard official United States policy in Indochina."[38] These "war trials" in Detroit, conducted by the VVAW, attacked both the justice of the war and the legitimacy of the narratives that undergird the military and militaristic nationalism.

2. *Community:* The second social gift of ritual is the spirit of unity and common affection. This takes place during the liminal or threshold stage and sometimes appears to be almost synonymous with liminality. "When people engage in ritual activity, they separate themselves, partially if not totally, from the roles and statuses they have in the workaday world. There is a threshold in time or space or both, and certainly a demarcation of behavior, over which people pass when entering into ritual. The day-to-day world, with its social structure, is temporarily suspended."[39] In this circumstance, separated from the normal system of social stratification with its designations of higher and lower, older and younger, inferior and superior, wise and ignorant, more powerful and less powerful, a different type of human bond may be experienced, "an essential and generic human bond"[40] that spans the distance created by structures that enhance either vertical or horizontal social separation.

Turner uses the term *communitas* to distinguish this spirit of unity from the geographical connotations of the word "community." A community (village, town, nation) enters into *communitas* only through ritual experiences that suspend the normal rules governing the way we feel and behave toward one another. This is both an ideal and an actual experience that occurs in the ritual process and is to be distinguished from mere social solidarity or common identity. Rituals of order like the Santa Fe ceremonies discussed above justify and reinforce social structures, thus assigning everyone her or his proper place in society.

Threshold rituals suspend the structures and create a spirit of affection and oneness that overcomes the potential or actual alienation of social structures. Presidential inauguration ceremonies were designed to achieve just such a sense of unity. Threshold experiences vary in intensity, running the gamut from an overwhelming experience of the holy (for example, Isaiah in the temple) and a complete turnaround of one's life (for example, the conversion of Saul on the Damascus Road) to the mild emotions one feels in a typical weekly service of worship. But whenever the liminal is involved, we glimpse a different order of things. Turner writes: "It is as though there are here two major 'models' for human interrelatedness, juxtaposed and alternating. The first is of society as a structured, differentiated, and often hierarchical system of politico-legal-economic positions with many types of evaluation, separating [people] in terms of 'more' or 'less.' The second, which emerges recognizably in the liminal period, is of society as ... [a] communion of equals who submit together to the general authority of the ritual elders."[41]

Turner puts so much emphasis on the second model that he regards all authentic rituals as bearers of *communitas*. Rites whose purpose is to maintain the hierarchical system (like those in Santa Fe mentioned above) he calls ceremonies. Those that once were bearers of *communitas* but are no longer, have degenerated into mere routines.

As his work progressed over the years, Turner expanded his concept of liminality. At first he considered liminality to be confined to that ritual moment when we are lifted out of the day-to-day structure of our social world. But as he concentrated more on the relationship between order and change and the various roles occupied by outsiders, marginals, and those in positions of structural inferiority, he enlarged the meaning of liminality to include "any condition outside or on the peripheries of everyday life."[42] At the same time he expanded the scope of liminality to include societal manifestations and liminal periods in history like the present, when the taken-for-granted assumptions of the Enlightenment have been shattered and old forms of social, economic, and political structure no longer appear viable. In this vein it is appropriate to regard the current crisis of American identity as a liminal period in our national history, provoked in large measure by the failure of our national narrative in Vietnam.

3. *Transformation:* We have explored the way in which ritual draws parentheses around certain moments in life and lifts us into a different sphere of being, in which the bonds of communal life are deepened by the temporary suspension of normal boundaries. Thus, the community-enhancing function of ritual is itself transformative. However, ritual also promotes change in at least two other ways.

First, it brings into being that which did not exist before. This is the major function of rites of passage: to lift a person or a group out of one status or condition and carry that person or group over into another. Whether it be a wedding, a graduation, a presidential inauguration, or a funeral, a ritual establishes that which did not exist in fullness before its performance. Something actually takes place in the world that changes the way we feel about ourselves and the way we relate to one another, as well as our legal status in the world. Our rights and responsibilities undergo change through such ritual. "Rites of passage always 'work,' since their enactment places their participants in a new social situation."[43] Recall the assassination of President Kennedy. For a brief time after his death in the Dallas hospital, the nation was without a president. This was a liminal moment filled with anxiety for many people. To allay fears and reestablish social order, Vice President Lyndon Johnson was installed almost immediately before returning to Washington on *Air Force 1*.[44]

The Vietnam-Era military is often criticized for not providing a rite of passage for soldiers leaving Vietnam. World War II GIs ended their war with a two-week return journey aboard ships, an extended rite of passage preparing them to return to civilian life. In contrast, the Vietnam "grunt" was whisked by jet from battle zone to hometown within a twenty-four-hour period, alone and without ceremony.

Rituals may also promote another type of change, an alteration of social structure itself. A rehearsal of the past can also be an implicit critical evaluation of the present, thereby generating hope by rehearsing an alternative future. "Cultural performances...may themselves be active agencies of change, representing the eye by which culture sees itself and the drawing board on which creative actors sketch out what they believe to be more apt or interesting 'designs for living.'"[45] The Winter Soldier Investigation referred to earlier is one example of the many ritualistic forms of protest enacted by various sectors of the antiwar movement.

Conclusion

Identity is the narrative out of which and into which we live. The narrative is in constant construction through conversation with multiple partners. These partners are located along three axes: length (tradition), breadth (social groups), and depth (self-reflection). Changes that occur along any one of these axes set off changes in the conversation itself. For many combat soldiers, the war experience so altered the self-reflection axis that their conversation with partners along the other two axes was radically interrupted. The next four chapters describe the dynamics of that process of radical interruption that amounts to the loss of a former identity.

Chapter Two

The Generic Vietnam War Narrative

It don't mean nothin'.
—Common litany of GIs in Vietnam

If I could see the fragments, know exactly what had happened to me and why, then when the ghosts whispered to me that it could have been different, I could prove them wrong.
—Jack Fuller, *Fragments*

The point of this is that we, gentlemen, we *have* to make some sense of this. We have to make some sense of ourselves.
—Charles Coleman, *Sergeant Back Again*

The Combat Soldier's Inner Experience

Only after the interview did I fully understand why the place of meeting was so important. A friend had put me in contact with a group of Vietnam veterans in a nearby town. They agreed to the interview, but it took four or five phone calls to decide on a place. Up to this point in my research I had been interviewing chaplains who had received treatment for post–traumatic stress disorder (PTSD) or therapists who were helping other vets work through their PTSD. For these professionals who could now distance themselves sufficiently from their own trauma to discuss the war without coming apart, the place of meeting was not particularly significant. But now when I invited

40

this group of combat vets to dinner, thinking that conversation over a meal would put them at ease for a discussion of delicate issues, they hedged. Sensing that I just didn't get it, one of them — John — explained, "When we start talking about the war, you never know what will happen."

So we selected a hideaway for our meeting, an isolated room at the back of the garden of a home owned by one of the vets. No onlookers, no phone, no interruptions. A safe place to explore once again the awful but fascinating horror of war. Rudolf Otto's depiction of the dual character of the experience of the holy — *mysterium tremendum et fascinans* (the daunting and fascinating mystery) — fits the combat soldier's experience of war.[1] War is horrible, yet it carries a magnetic fascination. It is an encounter so profound as to mark a person indelibly for life, an encounter that in some mysterious way can only be described as a numinous rite of passage. This early interview with combat vets prepared me for others like it, all journeys into sacred danger.

As discussed in the previous chapter, anthropologists describe the "liminal" or threshold stage in rites of passage. The initiate leaves one status in society (as if exiting over the threshold of a house), undergoes a period of training and testing, often with numinous overtones, and then crosses a new threshold into a different status in society. For combat soldiers war is a liminal experience, a rite of passage that wounds.[2] Those who come to terms with their wounds don't "tell war stories," for "telling war stories" is casting pearls before swine. It trivializes the experience and compromises the soldier's integrity.

The quotations at the beginning of this chapter capture the progression of a soldier's inner experience after being initiated or "blooded" into battle. During the heat of the war, things just don't add up. All is chance and chaos: why you were drafted and another was spared; why a buddy catches a round in the chest while you go unscathed; why a whole unit is wiped out by "friendly fire." On overload, your only defense against the apparent absurdities is to dismiss them with a turn of phrase, "It don't mean nothin'."

It actually means *everything*, but no one has figured out how to express it, and you are too busy just staying alive.[3] When you return home, you try to forget the war, but you can't. The more you repress it, the more the war wreaks its revenge via PTSD. You have entered a different world, and for you the old prewar world you left behind no longer exists. So like Morgan, the narrator of Jack Fuller's novel *Fragments*, you ask the surgeon for the pieces of shrapnel removed from your buttocks, and you turn them over and over in your hand, in your mind, trying to piece together the fragments of your shattered world.

Most trauma survivors go through an incubation or hibernation period before they can even begin to articulate the meaning of what has happened to them. It is not surprising that the best American literature on the Vietnam War did not emerge until ten to fifteen years after the authors' experiences in Southeast Asia. Gradually, though, the impulse to bear witness emerges. "We *have* to make some sense of this" becomes a sacred calling. When you reach this stage, you tell and retell the story because its meaning is manifold but elusive, and telling and retelling are the only ways to "get it right," to make some sense of it. But when you tell the story, you need a safe place and a sympathetic audience, because "you never can tell what will happen."

Elements of the
Generic Vietnam War Narrative

The claim that something called a "generic Vietnam War narrative" actually exists might at first glance appear dubious. The published memoirs and novels by American vets of the Vietnam War now number well over twelve hundred,[4] and each vet has a personal version, whether put in writing or passed on orally.

As noted earlier, from the standpoint of the participants there were in fact many wars in Vietnam, depending upon where and when one served and in what capacity. There are also conflicting ideological perspectives ranging from the very positive to the entirely negative.[5] Some write as propagandists for an American crusade. For the most part these stories are potboilers for popular titillation, following the hackneyed script of war as a young man's initiation into adulthood. These narratives use scapegoats to explain the outcome. Sometimes the press and the antiwar movement are fingered, or even the military itself. "Our government wouldn't let us win." This phrase usually refers to the restraints on the U.S. military that prevented it from invading North Vietnam with a slash-and-burn mandate or from bombing Hanoi "back into the Stone Age."

Other stories express the standard military point of view: war is hell, but necessary and honorable. It's a job that has to be done; someone has to do it; only "real men" are up to the task. In the center of the spectrum is the view that Vietnam can best be described as "a standard Shakespearean tragedy, in five acts, with a prologue and a rather ragged epilogue."[6] Further to the left is the view that the war was a terrible miscalculation, an aberration in the traditional anticolonial posture of American foreign policy. And finally there are those who regard Vietnam as the place where America was *rediscovered*,[7] the ultimate revelation of a "horror [that] had been implicit in the American character from the outset, . . . a prophetic curse hiding at the heart of a whole mythology of culture."[8]

Frequently, a vet's story will combine several of these perspectives with little attempt to disentangle them. These diverse perspectives call forth different genres of narratives from the fully realist to the entirely absurdist, and everything in between. The more imaginative narratives, like Tim O'Brien's *Going after Cacciato*[9] and Stephen Wright's *Meditations in Green*,[10] embody a number of genres in what are essentially philosophical quests for meaning.

In spite of the conflicting perspectives and diversity of styles, when we examine the common structure and themes of these stories a "generic" Vietnam War narrative does emerge, a story that one vet describes as "barely suppressed screams."[11] The structure of most narratives from any war is patterned on the archetypal hero myth involving a journey with three stages: preparation, battle, and recovery. In Vietnam the stages from "cherry" or FNG (fucking new guy)[12] to "short-timer" are marked by standard features: enlistment, basic training, the baptism of fire (first combat mission), the seductive thrill of battle, dismemberment and death of friends, growing callousness, the desire for revenge, atrocities, drug and sex scenes, intense brotherhood among the "grunts" but increasing conflict between the enlisted men and their officers, helicopter assaults, R & R, the countdown until DEROS (date of expected return from overseas), and finally the flight back to "the world" (the United States) and the hostile reception from fellow Americans.

Unique Features of the Vietnam War

The 365-Day Tour of Duty

Several characteristics of the Vietnam War set it apart from other American wars. The most prominent were the 365-day tour of duty (thirteen months for the marines) "in country" (Vietnam) and the strategy of attrition. The limited tour was designed to prevent the extensive shell shock that immobilized so many U.S. soldiers in previous wars. Its effect, however, was to individualize the war, weakening the cohesion of fighting units. Each soldier who joined a unit already stationed in Vietnam arrived alone and left alone. With 100 percent turnover per year in every unit, soldiers sometimes fought and died beside each other without even knowing one another's names. Survival eclipsed every other goal. Each day soldiers carefully scratched through another block on their personal short-time calendars. "They corrupted us with hope: Three hundred sixty-five days or life, whichever came first. Time was the enemy. Time was the objective. . . . The army counted corpses, but we counted days."[13]

The Strategy of Attrition

Previous American wars were fought for territory with a front and a rear. Not so in Vietnam. U.S. forces took a hill one day, with considerable losses, and abandoned it the next. Later, they repeated the same battle, with similar losses. Peasant farmers and enemy soldiers wore the same clothes, so that neither U.S. forces nor the ARVN (Army of the Republic of Vietnam) could be sure who was for them and who was against them. Sometimes the people who worked on American fire bases were friends by day and enemies by night. Even the children selling Coca Cola along the roadside were suspect. Since conquering territory served no purpose, the military adopted a policy of attrition. Success was measured in kill ratios (the proportion of enemy dead to one's own dead), calculated by daily body counts. If farmers ran when U.S. troops descended in helicopters, they were judged enemy and therefore fair game. To the "cherry's" question, "How do I know if they are VC [Vietcong soldiers]?" came the officer's response, "If they're dead, they're VC." One unit vied with another for a higher body count. Some units gave rewards — cold beer or extra time off — to those with the highest kill rates.

In one vet group I visited, three of the men had served as Special Forces (Green Berets) in the Phoenix program. "My job was to gather intelligence," said one. "I was a torturer." Another described his role in the assassination of suspected VC leaders. "I still see the eyes of the men I choked to death — the fierce and terrified eyes, how they change as life is slowly choked out of them." The third was silent until the end of the meeting, although his body language spoke loudly of inner turmoil. Finally he volunteered: "I murdered for *greed*. For the *fun* of it. To increase my number of kills." In a war of attrition soldiers gradually lose their moral bearings. Thus, the movement within Vietnam War narratives depicts a gradual deterioration of order, disintegration of moral character, alienation from the military establishment as well as from those at home, and the loss of all purpose save the will to survive.[14]

Language

The alienation and disintegration resulting from this war of attrition are portrayed by the subtle juxtaposition of three different types of language among vets: standard American English, official militarese, and conversational slang.[15] By shifting back and forth from one of these languages to another, the narrator conveys different settings, roles, and experiences. Standard American English is used for description, commentary, and reflection. The tone is objective, factual, somewhat distant. Jargon, technical terms, euphemisms, codes, and acronyms comprise a second language, official militarese. It is specific, realistic, disciplined, efficient, and highly denotative, well adapted to battle conditions where exactitude without emotion is essential for survival.

Conversational slang, a third form of expression, is almost the opposite of official militarese: rebellious, obscene, irreverent, ironic, ungrammatical, and highly connotative of the full range of emotional states. This language derives from the smart-aleck posturing of postadolescent males, the hard, stoic brutality of those trained to kill, and the personal — almost private — metaphoric slang of the Brotherhood, a slang heavily influenced by large numbers of African-American soldiers. Obscenity is a part of the survival code. In basic training drill sergeants use it to break down civilian identity and develop the meanness required of killers. Obscenity serves many purposes: to vent frustration and anger, to express irony and cynicism, to fuel courage and build esprit de corps, even to express respect and tenderness.[16] A central function is to overcome fear, as illustrated by the motto some soldiers inscribed on their flak jackets: "Yea, though I walk through the Valley of the Shadow of Death, I shall fear no Evil, because I'm the meanest motherfucker in the Valley."[17]

The obscenity of war stories is due in part, but only in part, to the cultural background of the majority of recruits and their socialization at boot camp. T. S. Eliot wrote of the occasional need of a writer to "dislocate" language to convey special meaning.[18] Vets use obscenity in this manner. It is an essential element of the soldier's witness. After a three-hour discussion with one veterans' group I asked, "What is the most important contribution that vets can make to American life?" Several people spoke at once: "Tell it like it was." "Don't pull any punches." "Speak the truth."

Because the war itself was obscene, only emotion-laden obscenity can even begin to convey the truth about the war. There is a macho callousness, a meanness, about these stories. Soldiers know they are in a forbidden zone. They have been systematically trained not only to kill but also to take pride in doing their job. The survival code reads, "Kill or be killed." And killing requires a certain meanness. Once the most sacred taboo of society — "Thou shalt not kill" — is reversed, a moral inversion occurs that infects other taboos as well. Restraints on other appetites — for sex, drugs, violence — lose their hold. The denigration of women, the atrocities visited upon the civilian population, racist hatred of enemy "gooks," and the "fragging"[19] of one's own officers can be traced in part to the survival code and the breach of the fundamental social taboo, "Thou shalt not kill." For reflective soldiers who glimpse in themselves and in others their moral deterioration, only obscenity can begin to convey the repulsive rot of war.

Obscenity is also a counterpoint to official militarese. In fact, militarese gives birth to obscenity.[20] Militarese is technical, objective, ordered, clinical, as if the chain of command had invented clean euphemisms to shield itself from the brutalities of the battlefield. In a world of moral inversion it is the euphemisms that are obscene because they mask the awful truth. At some point in a war of attrition, combat soldiers are seized by the revelation that to the commanders back in Saigon and Washington they are expendable cannon fodder, mere "meat," valued only in terms of kill ratios. The VC attack and a buddy is decapitated. After the battle you remove the body from a large pool of blood. Before you can zip up the body bag, you vomit. When the casualty officer makes the report, he describes the cause of death in militarese, "traumatic amputation," giving the impression of a surgical operation.[21] Such euphemisms deepen your sense of betrayal.[22] To "tell it like it was" requires the angry repudiation of militarese, the use of raw language to describe the obscenities of the system itself.

The Disintegration of the American Mythic Landscape

A more basic feature that distinguished the Vietnam War from previous wars was the early disintegration of the American worldview or what literary critics call the "mythic landscape." This mythic landscape is the essential framework of the classic American narrative. It was originally expressed with religious metaphors (the chosen people, the New Israel, a city set on a hill, a light to the nations, an errand into the wilderness, the pilgrim saints versus the native savages), but by the mid–twentieth century these had been replaced by secularized counterparts: the frontier, cowboys and Indians, Manifest Destiny, the Free World. Whether religious or secular, these metaphors share a common character: the Manichaean opposition of good and evil. In 1960 and 1961, John F. Kennedy, following the pattern set by Truman and Eisenhower before him, situated his presidency and the cold war struggle with international communism within this traditional American Manichaean mythos.[23]

In the years since World War II, the Soviet Union had

achieved nuclear parity with the United States and had won the first round of the space race with the launching of *Sputnik;* China had fallen to Mao Tse-tung; a bloody stalemate in Korea cost dearly; communist insurgency was threatening elsewhere in Asia; and Khrushchev was promising massive Soviet support for "wars of liberation." In 1958, William Lederer, a recently retired special assistant to the Pacific commander in chief, and Eugene Burdick, a professor of political science at Berkeley, published a novel, *The Ugly American,*[24] which shaped the national debate over American identity for the next decade. It went through twenty printings in five months and was on the best-seller lists for twenty-seven months, arresting the attention of the nation's policymakers. The novel is situated in the center of the classic national mythic landscape of American innocence, power, and destiny. The American decline in the 1950s vis-à-vis the communist world was due to the corruption of the American character, Lederer and Burdick claimed, and to a loss of the historic national mission. This premise formed the backdrop of the 1960 presidential election.

In 1961 the newly elected president responded to the challenge within this traditional mythical framework. His New Frontier included a physical fitness program to recover national youth and vigor, a revitalized U.S. space program, an "alliance for progress" with Latin American countries, and the creation of the Peace Corps and the Special Forces (Green Berets). The Peace Corps would combat communism by assisting poor countries in capitalist development schemes; the Green Berets would thwart communist guerrillas by counterinsurgency, the form of warfare proposed in *The Ugly American.* Kennedy called upon Americans to "bear any burden" on behalf of the national mission. The young men of America responded eagerly, swelling the ranks of the military. "War is always attractive to young men who know nothing about it," writes Philip Caputo, "but we had also been seduced into uniform by Kennedy's challenge to 'ask what you can do for your country' and by the missionary idealism he had awakened in us."[25]

The very language used by the military in Vietnam conveyed pictures of the mythic landscape of the Indian wars nurtured by Hollywood westerns. The brass explained the mission in Manichaean terms as a battle between civilization and savagery, and the Green Berets, our idealized self-image — and lineal descendants of the rugged, pure-hearted Indian fighter/frontiersman — fulfilled the prophecy. These modern-day Daniel Boones (the small units of Special Forces that made excursions into Cambodia in the late 1960s and early 1970s were called Daniel Boone teams) embraced savage means to achieve civilization's goals. Most U.S. combat soldiers regarded Vietnamese as an inferior breed of "gooks," "slopes," or "dinks." Some early maps included a "Dodge City" with the land beyond described as "Indian country." Dense forests were regarded as wilderness (free-fire zones) to be cleared (defoliated). U.S. policy called for the establishment of garrisons and reservations (strategic hamlets). Officers ordered their men to "saddle up" before leaving their firebase. As on stagecoaches, someone "rode shotgun" on most vehicles. Vietnamese interpreters working with U.S. units were called Kit Carson scouts and sometimes given names like Apache. "Come on," a captain said to newsman Michael Herr, inviting him to accompany his unit on a search-and-destroy mission. "We'll take you out to play cowboys and Indians." When the unit killed an unarmed Vietnamese, they labeled him a "scout." "They couldn't even tell for sure," writes Herr, "whether he was from a friendly tribe or not, no markings on his arrows because his quiver was empty, like his pockets and his hands."[26]

The narratives are replete with references to this mythic landscape. Although "John Wayne" quickly became a verb and a term of derision in Vietnam — grunts accused one another of "John Wayning" when they took unnecessary risks or played the hero — the mythic framework disintegrated only gradually. At first the problem was diagnosed in terms of too few cowboys with insufficient gunpowder, so year by year the number of U.S. troops increased: from 23,000 in 1964 to 543,000 in 1969. By then, however, it was clear to the most perceptive combat soldiers that the American scenario had failed in Vietnam and that instead of riding into the sunset in glory, Americans had taken on the evil characteristics of the communist "savages" they had come to annihilate.

Reasons for Telling the Story

Getting the Story Right

If there is such similarity among these narratives, we might ask why veterans keep telling them and why the public keeps listening. Of course much of the American public has never listened, and this fact itself is enough to spur the vets to continue their witness until they are heard. Even so, the audience has expanded. One answer is that in spite of the generic features, each narrative puts a particular spin on the experience of war. The form of fictional narratives ranges from faithful realism to unrelenting absurdism, an indication that veterans have different assessments of the meaning of those experiences that they share. And these meanings continue to change.

I asked one minister why he joined the military chaplaincy. "At one time I thought I knew," he said, "but the more I reflect on it the more my reasons change." This may explain why good writers frequently write several narratives on the war. The experience is so porous, so multilayered, and so mysterious that each time it is told and each time it is heard, new meaning emerges. Since the most profound experiences are generally described in rich, metaphorical, and multivalent language — the conversational slang of grunts — the hearers or readers are drawn into the story and must decipher meaning for themselves.

The imperative to "get it right" becomes a joint venture of storyteller and audience.

Catharsis

A second reason for the continued expansion of this literature is the cathartic value of testimony. It's as if the storyteller has become a prisoner of war whose release will be achieved only through faithful witness. In spite of the diversity of contexts, which lends variety, the common thread that runs through the best narratives is the confusion, absurdity, and horror of "barely suppressed screams." Robert Mason was a helicopter pilot in Vietnam in 1965 and 1966. He flew over one thousand combat missions in one year, each time wondering if the landing zone would be "hot" (under enemy fire) and whether he would live to fly again. He was eyewitness to the carnage and mayhem of repeated battles, carting away the bodies of the mutilated. Upon his return to the United States he became a flight instructor at Fort Wolters, Texas, but was grounded after some time because he suffered persistent post–traumatic stress. When his nightmares became too intense he escaped into alcohol, until he required a bottle a day along with tranquilizers. "If I stayed drunk, I could cope. When I was sober, life was unending anxiety with no focus."[27]

One particular nightmare kept haunting him night after night. He told the VA psychiatrist:

> Every morning the truck comes. I have to open the door; I know what's out there, but I still go to the door. It's always the same. The driver backs the truck to the door and says, "How many do you want?" He points to a truck of babies. Dead babies. I always gag at the sight. They all look dead, but then I see an eyelid blink in the pile, then another. Then I always answer, "Two hundred pounds, Jake." I laugh when I say it. Jake picks up a pitchfork and stabs it into the pile and drops a couple of corpses on a big scale.

"Nearly ten pounds a head," he says. Inside my head I'm yelling for him to stop, that the babies aren't dead, but Jake just keeps loading the scale. Each time he stabs a kid, it squirms on the fork, but Jake doesn't notice a thing.[28]

Mason continued to suffer from post–traumatic stress for well over a decade after his return from Vietnam, unable to find release through therapy or contentment in any business venture he attempted. His wife and friends urged him to write about Vietnam, recognizing that unless he found a way to relive the traumatic war experiences and come to terms with them, they would haunt him for the rest of his life. The Mason family moved to rural Florida, where together Robert and his wife, Patience, worked a paper route to make ends meet while he wrote his way out of Vietnam. In 1981, still on alcohol and drugs, he was charged with smuggling marijuana into the country and sentenced to five years at a minimum security prison. There he finished the manuscript of *Chickenhawk*, one of the most riveting narratives on the helicopter air war in Vietnam.

Other vets experience similar healing by recording their own war experience or by writing fictional accounts of the war. Personal catharsis through storytelling is more than mere release of emotional tensions. It is a creative act reconstituting the self. Basic training removes recruits from the civilian world and thrusts upon them a new identity. After the war vets are faced with crossing another threshold — back into society. The new status requires shedding the warrior personality and creating a whole new postwar self. If the liminal experience of battle is traumatic, the personality is permanently altered. The survivor remains somewhat separate, a marked person, whose reintegration takes the form of public witness.[29]

Trauma survivors who have reexperienced and worked through their travail have a compulsion to tell and retell the story, each time mining the trauma for new and deeper

revelatory insights. Elie Wiesel explains the Holocaust survivor's compulsion: "I never intended to be a philosopher
or a theologian. The only role I sought was witness. I believed that, having survived by chance, I was duty-bound
to give meaning to my survival, to justify each moment
of my life. I knew the story had to be told. Not to trans-
mit an experience is to betray it."[30] A similar urgency
permeates the narratives of the Vietnam War. Survivors
are storytellers with a mission. "You were Lazarus back
from the dead," says the narrator in *Fragments*, "and you
needed to report what you had seen."[31] Herein lies a clue
to the popularity of the war literature, in spite of the similarities among the various narrative accounts. The good
narratives have an intensity to them, a ring of authentic
truth-telling, a story that is urgent. The reader is drawn
in, engaged, challenged to cry out with the author, "Never
again!" Implicit in this cry is the plea for forgiveness: "Yes,
you wanted them to understand because they were your
jury; they had sent you off to war, and now that you had
returned, they alone had the power to honor and excuse."[32]

Sense-Making

Storytelling derives from another impulse that is perhaps
even stronger than the need for catharsis and social engagement. Viktor Frankl, whose work was described in
chapter 1, calls it the "will to meaning." This powerful
need to make sense of experience accounts for the drive
in Vietnam War stories to go beyond mimetic realism —
the tell-it-like-it-was impulse — to explore the parabolic
dimensions of the war.

Occasionally in a narrative the author will include a disclaimer, indicating that his is a personal story that has little
to do with the larger political issues for which the war was
fought. Philip Caputo begins *A Rumor of War* with such a
disclaimer: "This book does not pretend to be history. It has
nothing to do with politics, power, strategy, influence, national interests, or foreign policy; nor is it an indictment

of the great men who led us into Indochina and whose mistakes were paid for with the blood of some quite ordinary men. In a general sense, it is simply a story about war, about the things men do in war and the things war does to them."[33] Such disclaimers have led some to conclude that Vietnam War narrators are narcissistic, overly influenced by existentialism, and uninterested in the larger sense-making task.[34]

This is an erroneous conclusion. It is understandable that veterans who were ignored, rejected, spit upon, and called baby-killers upon their return to the United States might be hesitant to enter into the fray of political controversy. Many did so by joining the antiwar movement. But once the war was over other Americans wanted to avoid further divisiveness and to nurse the domestic wounds that had been festering for so long. What better way for veterans to contribute to the long-term debate over the legacies of the war than to write about what they knew best, their own 365-day tour "in country"? Thus the impression that war narratives are merely personal stories is deceptive. By depicting in concrete specificity the absurdities of the war from the perspective of the combat soldier, they are at the same time calling indirect attention to the foreign policy, the national interests, the military strategy, and the worldview that led to American intervention in Southeast Asia. In short, they are calling attention to the impact of the war on the meaning and purpose of America.

The intensity of the sense-making imperative is proportionate to the depth of disillusionment that the vet has experienced. In the early years of American involvement, when domestic support for the war was still strong, most GIs tended to go along with government explanations. They knew that counterinsurgency was different from conventional warfare and could not always be judged by the same standards. The crusade against communism was still sufficient to justify the ambiguities they had to face. However, even some of the first regular troops to see action in Vietnam began to question the war after a few months of combat. By the end of 1965, when U.S. troop level was at 180,000, up from 23,000 a year earlier, it was evident to some that America was stuck in a quagmire, with goals that could not be achieved.[35] As the war dragged on and the antiwar movement cranked up in the United States, GIs found it harder to believe official justifications for the war. Profound disillusionment spread throughout the troops. Veterans who write about the late 1960s and early 1970s find sense-making more difficult. Jack Fuller's novel *Fragments* is a prime example of the shattering of meaning during this period.

The Fragging of America

The setting of *Fragments* is late 1968 and early 1969, after the VC (Vietcong) and the NVA (North Vietnamese Army) regulars had inflicted stunning casualties during the Tet Offensive of January–February 1968. Tet was the psychological turning point of the war. During the offensive, twenty-eight of the forty-eight cities and provincial capitals in South Vietnam were attacked, many simultaneously. The surprising enemy strength gave the lie to official U.S. prophecies of a "light at the end of tunnel" and further demoralized U.S. troops. Into the midst of this disillusionment strides big Jim Neumann, the protagonist of *Fragments*, the quintessential 1960s version of the all-American hero. His story can be understood as an ironic parable of the self-inflicted fragmentation of American identity and purpose.

Most of the generic elements mentioned above are present at one point or another as the narrator, Sergeant Morgan, takes the reader on his journey from basic training to war and back home again. Although the pattern and the action of this story are mimetic in style, the emotional tone is different from that of the typical realist novel. Rather than reproducing the highs and lows of actual war experiences, Fuller's tone is more reflective, more philosophical.

The novel was first published in 1984, indicating perhaps that by then the author had worked through the intense emotional traumas of war but had yet to make sense of the experience. His purpose is not so much to provide the reader with a feel for vivid action as to examine the pieces of evidence from a war that shattered all meaning. A doctor tells the wounded Morgan after surgery, "Any fragments that are still in there will work themselves to the surface in time" (p. 26). By means of a parabolic narrative the author encourages us to piece together the fragments lodged in our corporate existence that are still working their way toward the surface of our common life.

The quote on the frontispiece of *Fragments,* from Paul Ricoeur's *Freedom and Nature,* provides a hint of the enigmatic philosophical knot that the book seeks to untie: "Wise [people] have always construed the recognition of necessity as a moment of freedom." So the issue is the tension between chance and necessity, on the one hand, and freedom and responsibility, on the other. The main characters represent abstract principles embodied in laconic but subtle personalities. Bill Morgan, the narrator, is opposed to the war from the beginning but reports for induction when he is drafted because "when you came from where I did, when you'd been raised on certain tales, when you'd learned to respect your father and his friends, not because of what they did in the wars but rather because of what they suffered, then you simply had no alternative when your number came up....It wasn't duty or honor or country or any lofty imperative. It had nothing to do with courage, moral or otherwise. It was simply who you were" (p. 29). Morgan, then, represents nature, chance, necessity: the absence of freedom and responsibility, praise and blame. He speaks for all those who regard war as evil but necessary, a job to be done. In him echoes the refrain of all those who claim, "Somebody's gotta do it. I was just following orders."

At the same time Morgan recognizes that there is "something seductive about surrendering to forces outside your control, beyond choice or blame" (p. 53). If you surrender to the forces, you might go too far, be carried away, begin enjoying the war. "You not only had to know how to kill, you had to know when and why, or else you were going to destroy yourself, too" (p. 57). This insight might be a reference to My Lai, which occurred in March of 1968, or to similar atrocities. Two characters in *Fragments* surrender to these forces: Thompson collects body parts from enemy corpses, and an unnamed suicidal grunt returns to Vietnam for a third tour because "once you've been gone, you can't *ever* come back" (p. 218).

In boot camp at Fort Bragg, Morgan establishes a deep friendship with his philosophical opposite, Jim Neumann, who has volunteered for Vietnam because of his restless energy and desire to maintain control over his own destiny. The very name Neumann (new human being) carries overtones of freedom, purity, and control enshrined in the "New Adam" of American mythology. Neumann represents what has traditionally been considered the best in America. He is tall, blond, physically fit but without any hint of swagger. A natural leader endowed with "can-do" optimism, he inspires courage and hope in others. Blacks regard Neumann as a "bro" and gather around him in the evenings as he plays the blues on his flute. He is gentle with children, kind to women, respectful of his enemies, a reluctant warrior who kills only when necessary and prohibits the maiming of corpses. Neumann relies not on chance and necessity but on freedom, initiative, and responsibility, elements of American self-confidence. "He simply refused to believe that there was anything that would not shape itself to the will" (p. 51). In spite of the disillusionment that was setting in among U.S. troops at this time in the war, Morgan reports that "every one of us saw something of himself in Neumann — the best part magnified" (p. 20).

The plot turns on an event in the village of Xuan The. The village, a few miles from his base camp, has been "adopted" by Neumann, perhaps to atone for the lives of those he has had to kill and also to release his boundless energy and give expression to the American need to help. At first the only goal is to rebuild a dilapidated dispensary left by the French. But gradually Neumann turns into a development planner with proposals for a full-scale reorganization of village life, including the introduction of a new division of labor, a second annual rice crop with imported hybrid rice seeds, the redirection of a river to form a moat around the village, and the erection of lights powered by an army generator to provide protection against the VC/NVA.

Neumann then falls in love with a young Vietnamese woman, Tuyet, and is welcomed by her mother, who herself has a young Amerasian son from an earlier incursion of American soldiers. Morgan warns Neumann that such attention from the Americans will make Xuan The a target for the enemy, but Neumann pays no heed. He plans to marry Tuyet and bring her back to the United States after his tour of duty. Meanwhile, he is bent on "improving" village life: "We have to leave them something. . . . We can't just come here, get all warm inside about how good we are, and then walk out on them. They are fine people. We have to make a difference" (p. 170). He envisions Xuan The as an "outpost," a "fort in the wilderness."

One morning the lieutenant awakens Morgan, Neumann, and the others with news that a U.S. helicopter has been downed by enemy fire at Xuan The. Their unit must investigate. When Neumann reaches the village, he runs for Tuyet's *hootch* (house), where he is surprised by a VC guerrilla. For the first time in the war he is faced with a situation beyond his understanding or control. He reverts to the reflexes he has learned in training and kills the guerrilla, Tuyet, her mother, and her baby brother. NVA machine guns pin down the Americans while mortars stalk their position. The lieutenant is killed; both Morgan and Neumann are wounded.

Later, at the military inquiry into the deaths of Tuyet and her family, Neumann is dumb, broken. "His eyes were as empty as a blind man's" (p. 20). Because the evidence is so fragmentary, the issue is dropped, but Morgan the narrator muses, "Not guilty is not the same thing as innocent" (p. 206). Morgan learns from Apache, the "Vietnamese Kit Carson scout," what Neumann had no way of knowing: the guerrilla in the *hootch* with Tuyet was her brother, who had been conscripted by the VC but had fled to Xuan The with the intention of defecting to the Americans.

Morgan is haunted with questions, and so are we. How could this New Adam fall so low, go over the edge, lose control, murder the woman he loved, destroy a village while trying to save it? What went wrong in that *hootch*? How could our best men act like our worst? Morgan dreams night after night: "Tuyet's happy face, the dispensary open for business, Neumann holding the hand of a child. Ghosts. They whispered to me that it could have been different. And I woke up screaming no" (p. 25).

Back in "the world," Morgan is obsessed with locating Neumann. Only Neumann can fit the fragments together and restore Morgan's faith. "If I could just talk to him, I know he could explain why it had to happen the way it did" (p. 246). But doubts about Neumann (and, by extension, about America) will not go away. "He had gone out in search of who he was. And baby, he had found it all right. He had touched the rotten center of it. I still believed in Jim Neumann, but it was hard. It was hard" (pp. 212–13).

When Morgan finally finds Neumann on a farm in downstate Illinois, Neumann is just as confused as everyone else. Did the guerrilla have a rifle, or was he unarmed? Was Tuyet cheating on him? Had she lied to him? Was his failure that he trusted too much or not enough? Or did he kill them because he "was losing them" (p. 283)? "I don't even know what I did. It's all falling apart. I can't remember it right.... Can't even *remember*" (p. 283).

In the end we are left with only fragments of an American identity that has been shattered, a national mission that has exploded in our faces. Now that we have "touched

the rotten center" of it, America, like Morgan and Neumann and all the others in their unit, must wait until all
the fragments come to the surface before the full meaning
of Vietnam can be pieced together.

Chapter Three

The Heart of Darkness

Nobody asks us why we're smiling because nobody
wants to know....To carry death in your smile, that
is ugly.
— Gustav Hasford, *The Short-Timers*

Our Love Affair with Violence

After the local Vietnam Veterans of America chapter meeting four of us withdrew to a smaller room. We exchanged
a few pleasantries and one of the men apologized for a fellow vet's outburst during the meeting. Then I asked each
one — Joe, Bill, and Ed — when they served in Vietnam
and where they were stationed. "I went in fresh out of college," said Ed, "in the mid '60s. Biggest adventure of my
life. Saw lots of action, search and destroy....I was just
like John Paul Vann,[1] gung ho the whole time." "Not me,"
Bill interrupted. "I didn't get to Nam until the early '70s.
Drafted. Even let my hair grow long and wore a peace symbol. Caught hell for it, but what could they do? Send me to
Vietnam? Most of the guys in my unit were disillusioned."
I shifted my eyes to Joe. "Me? I was a surgeon at division
headquarters," Joe replied. "I saw a lot of shit, a real-life
M*A*S*H scene, but I got along OK. In fact, I had a pretty
good time. When I left they had a party for me and gave
me this plaque." Joe holds out an engraved, metal-on-wood
plaque. "It was only later that things fell apart for me."
  The conversation continued like this for several hours,
each one answering my questions with stories from his

62

time in Vietnam and, since then, back in the States. One subject kept coming up again and again: violence. The violence of the war, violence on television and in the movies, "America's love affair with violence," as Ed put it with angry sarcasm in his voice. At one point Bill turned to Ed and asked, "You ever spank your children?" "Only one time — my oldest." Not catching the deeper significance, I queried Bill. "Why did you ask that question?" "Because we know what can happen if we lose control, the violence that resides within our souls. That's what we learned about ourselves in Vietnam. Ed has four children, all under twelve years old. He's a good father. He's only lost it one time." He paused and looked down at the floor. Then in a hushed voice he continued. "I've spanked my kids three times. It terrified me for weeks afterward."

A silence descended upon us as each man withdrew a bit into his own reveries. After a while Bill took a deep breath, looked at the floor, and leaned forward in his chair. "I...I have something to say," he began in a soft, quaking voice. "I never told you before. Not in all those years we spent together in the rap group. I've never told anyone."

We waited while Bill shifted again in his chair, wringing his hands and taking quick, short breaths. "They put me on garbage detail as punishment, because they knew that I can't stand flies. One day I was hauling the garbage to the dump. This little Vietnamese friend, Chu, jumped into the jeep with me. I was glad to see him. He always cheered me up. When we got to the dump I took all the bottles and smashed them, one by one in the dump. A big mound of broken beer bottles. Gettin' my anger out. Chu kept turning over the garbage, looking for food and anything else he could salvage. It was stirring up flies, so I told him to clear out. He laughed and paid no attention. When the flies swarmed all over me, I lost it. I picked him up and slammed him down on that mound of broken glass. He screamed and I got into the jeep and drove away." Bill closed his eyes as tears ran down his face. "I can see him now, one mass of blood spurting all over the glass. I don't know whether he lived or died."

Bill slumped back into his chair, eyes still closed, hands covering his wet face. Joe reached out and put a hand on Bill's arm. We remained silent for a long time. Finally, as if to bring closure to the painful revelation, Ed looked at me and said, "That's our love affair with violence."

The classic American narrative includes the myth of regeneration by violence.[2] In the movie version the virile hero is by nature gentle and kind, having renounced the use of guns. But when the forces of evil threaten the frontier community he reluctantly, but also with a certain degree of pleasure, takes the law into his own hands and redeems the community *from* violence *by* violence. This narrative is as fresh as Desert Storm. The military relies on this idealized masculine role. Without it, the task of turning civilians into soldier-killers would be much more difficult. When he took command of the Third Army in England in 1944, General George S. Patton, Jr., addressed his troops: "The third reason we are fighting [the first was to preserve liberties; the second, to defeat the Nazis] is because men like to fight.... Men like to fight, and if they don't, they're not real men."[3] The secret kept from young soldiers is the price they must pay for embracing violence. Combat veterans who served in Vietnam know the secret, for they have entered the darkness where the secret is kept. There they met evil, face to face.

Liminality

To understand the self-destructive vortex of violence that engulfed U.S. combat soldiers in Vietnam, we will rely upon three interrelated concepts: liminality, the descent into the heart of darkness, and abjection. We shall deal with the first two in this chapter and the last in chapter 4. We have already examined the concept of liminality in chapter 2 in the context of our discussion of rites of passage. Here we must underscore one essential feature of the threshold or liminal period in a rite of passage: it is a *dangerous* period during which the normal rules of behavior, including strict taboos, are set aside or even transposed into their opposites.

The journey from civilian to soldier and back to civilian is a rite of passage writ large. Looked at from this overarching perspective, the entire military career of volunteers and draftees who do not reenlist can be regarded as the liminal period. Within the period of military service itself the most dramatic liminal experience occurs during combat when the normal taboos that restrain violence are themselves violated. This is a particularly dangerous period because skillful use of the techniques of violence is necessary for self-*defense*, but excessive violence is self-*destructive*. In words quoted earlier: "You not only had to know how to kill, you had to know when and why, or else you were going to destroy yourself, too."[4]

To perform under fire a soldier needs to "psyche up" until he reaches "the edge," that state of readiness so familiar to every athlete, a state that involves an exhilarating rush of adrenaline and a mixture of fear, courage, skill, and sometimes meanness. But once a soldier climbs to "the edge," it takes only a little nudge to "lose it," to go "over the edge." Vets call this "going over to the dark side." For some, like Bill in the interview reported above, this is only momentary, followed by remorse and confusion and sometimes the loss of effectiveness as a soldier. Others recognize that "going over to the dark side" assists them in combat and is to be desired rather than resisted, so that it becomes a permanent expression of their new identity.

The abrupt and temporary loss of control is also accompanied by a gradual process of internal deterioration. Figure 5 captures this process.[5] The price paid for this new dehumanized identity is best understood by the metaphor of descent into the heart of darkness.

Figure 5

Descent into the Heart of Darkness

We noted earlier that war stories most frequently follow the tripartite pattern of archetypal hero myths involving preparation, battle, and recovery. This is the traditional journey to the underworld in Greek myth or the descent into hell made famous by Dante's *Divine Comedy*. Vietnam War stories differ from the traditional pattern in that paradise is lost, but not regained. Rather than follow Dante's pattern, these stories are more often modeled after Joseph Conrad's novella *Heart of Darkness*.[6]

The typical GI began his tour of duty with visions of John Wayne, the quintessential American hero, dancing in his head. By the early 1960s John Wayne had become an icon, the warrior-gentleman, representing American masculinity. He had played the part of every cultural hero, embodying patriotic mission, courage, toughness, honor, confidence, leadership and so forth. He was fearless under fire, eager for battle, always in control. In his battles of good versus evil there was little room for fear or doubt or moral complexity.[7]

In several Vietnam novels and memoirs, GIs are seated in an open-air theater at a firebase in Vietnam watching a John Wayne movie when their first Vietcong mortar attack begins. Even late in the war when many GIs were already thoroughly disillusioned and when "Don't try any John Waynes" had become a stock warning to new recruits, recreation programs at U.S. base camps all over Vietnam still showed John Wayne films. Tobey Herzog reports that at Long Binh in January 1970 he and his unit were watching *The Green Berets* when a mortar attack sent them scurrying for their bunkers. "Safely inside, I realize that even from my perspective as a clerk in a relatively secure area, the Vietnam War is not following the typical Hollywood script of a John Wayne movie, especially *The Green Berets*. "[8]

Instead of the John Wayne script of order, control, and progress, American GIs experienced a descent into chaos and savagery. Conrad's *Heart of Darkness* is the prototype used by many for interpreting the Vietnam experience. In fact, a simple substitution of terminology in reading this novella (American for European and Vietnamese for African) leaves us marveling at Conrad's uncanny prescience. Thus, a word about this story should be helpful.

In 1890, at the age of thirty-three, Conrad accomplished one of his childhood dreams by sailing up the Congo River into the heart of Africa. He was appalled by what he discovered. Under the sponsorship of King Leopold I of Belgium and in the name of the European "civilizing mission," agents of the Société Anonyme Belge pour le Commerce du Haut-Congo were enslaving, maiming, and killing the local inhabitants to satisfy an insatiable greed for ivory. This experience was so disturbing that a nine-year gestation period was necessary before the novella *Heart of Darkness* was written and published. In the book Conrad explores the dynamics of evil and illustrates what is commonly recognized by writers who are Vietnam veterans — that fiction is often the most appropriate vehicle for laying bare the inner meaning of factual, historical experience. The parallels between this novella and the American war in Vietnam are so striking that Francis Coppola, in his film *Apocalypse Now,* interprets the Vietnam War as America's modern version of *Heart of Darkness.* At the symbolic level, this metaphor unveils the inner meaning of that war better than any other.

One evening aboard a yawl anchored in the Thames River as darkness descends upon them, Charlie Marlow recounts to four companions his experience as captain of a "Company" steamer engaged in the ivory trade on the Congo River. The journey from the "Company Station" near the Atlantic coast to the "Inner Station" one thousand miles inland — where Kurtz, the most prolific ivory hunter, is engaged in barbarous acts — is described with irony and double entendres. Perhaps Conrad's title was influenced by Henry Morton Stanley's famous account of his explorations of the Congo, *In Darkest Africa,* published in 1890, for Marlow displays the prevailing ethnocentric European attitudes toward "primitives" and "savages," and the jungle wilderness serves as a metaphor for darkness. The farther Marlow enters into the jungle the more he is ensnared by the tentacles of evil.

Conrad's real subject, however, is the potential for evil that resides in every human heart and the actual darkness that lies at the heart of "civilization," a sinister darkness — born of hypocrisy and self-righteousness — that has been projected onto Africans and then used as an excuse for conquest and exploitation. Marlow's aunt in Brussels, who secures him the ship-captain's job with the ivory company, views him as "an emissary of light" in the effort to wean "those ignorant millions from their horrid ways."[9] The ivory agents refer to the "noble cause," the "cause of progress," and one, the brickmaker, refers to Kurtz as "a prodigy," "an emissary of pity, and science, and progress," with "higher intelligence, wide sympathies, a singleness of purpose," dedicated to "the guidance of the cause entrusted to us by Europe" (p. 40). Kurtz himself, a gifted rhetorician given to "splendid monologues on love, justice, conduct of life" (p. 74), is a virtuoso poet of European idealism who wishes to make "each station...a beacon on the road towards better things, a center for trade of course, but also for humanising, improving, instructing" (p. 47).

Marlow, who has visited the death grove of those exhausted from their slave labor, observes the hypocrisy and self-deception cloaked by the notion of the "noble cause," and he describes the human degradation resulting from it. Upon reflection, "the conquest of the earth, which mostly means the taking it away from those who have a different complexion or slightly flatter noses than ourselves, is not a pretty thing when you look into it too much" (p. 21). In fact, the greed and other passions underlying this conquest give off an odor of death. "The word 'ivory' rang in the air, was whispered, was sighed. You would think they were praying to it. A taint of imbecile rapacity blew through it all, like a whiff from some corpse" (p. 37).

Marlow wonders: If the "noble cause" is in reality so odious, how can honorable, self-respecting people give themselves over to it? He discovers the answer in the human ability to transform ideals into idols that mask the horrors and calm the conscience of the conqueror. "What redeems it is the idea only. An idea at the back of it; not a sentimental pretence but an idea; and an unselfish belief in the idea — something you can set up, and bow down before, and offer a sacrifice to" (p. 21). Thus, virtue and vice

commingle in intimate proximity, the former becoming the
vehicle of the latter.

Marlow had originally taken the job to fulfill a childhood dream of exploring a part of the globe that was not
yet filled in on the maps. As he journeys toward the "Inner
Station," Marlow discovers that his original motivation has
changed. Now he is obsessed with meeting Kurtz, who,
Marlow realizes, is mad. In his desire to make a name for
himself, Kurtz has renounced every constraint and broken
every taboo in the all-consuming quest for more and more
ivory. Separated from the laws and restraints of his own
society, alone in the wilderness and possessing superior
firepower, Kurtz has "kicked himself loose of the earth"
(p. 82). He has become a law unto himself, with no faith
and no fear, a god receiving worship and sacrifice from
those he rules and whom he uses to raid other tribes in
the rapacious hunt for ivory.

Marlow interrupts the story at one point to warn his
companions against any self-righteous judgment of Kurtz.
"You can't understand. How could you? — with solid
pavement under your feet, surrounded by kind neighbours
ready to cheer you or to fall on you, stepping delicately
between the butcher and the policeman, in the holy terror of scandal and gallows and lunatic asylums — how
can you imagine what particular region of the first ages
a man's untrammelled feet may take him into by the
way of solitude — utter solitude without a policeman —
by the way of silence — utter silence, where no warning
voice of a kind neighbour can be heard whispering public
opinion?" (p. 64).

In his ethnographic approach to the psychology of colonization, Octave Mannoni describes the isolation of the colonizer from the colonized. Separated by culture, language,
and religion from creatures considered to be inferior, and
possessing superior weaponry, the colonizer regards the
colonized as "Other."[10] The inequality of the relationship
renders impossible any genuine understanding between
the two because reciprocity, the foundation of true com-

munication, is absent. As a result, the colonizers are free to project their own darkness onto the Other and then proceed to destroy the Other, all in the name of the noble cause.

When the steamer finally arrives, Kurtz is ill and the Inner Station in decay. In front of the dilapidated house is a row of posts with a human head stuck on each one, drying in the sun. The unfinished seventeen-page manuscript Kurtz has written for the future guidance of the International Society for the Suppression of Savage Customs vibrates with altruistic eloquence, but at the bottom of the last page are scrawled these words: "Exterminate all the brutes!" (pp. 65–66). An abrupt switch from noble self-sacrifice to indiscriminate genocide.

Marlow recognizes that Kurtz has become the darkness, that "the wilderness . . . had whispered to him things about himself which he did not know, . . . and the whisper had proved irresistibly fascinating" (p. 73). Having deceived himself into justifying evil in the name of good, Kurtz has discovered the evil within himself and become fascinated by it, giving it free reign. And it is killing him, devouring him from within. Kurtz is divided by a "strange commingling of desire and hate" (p. 86). A war rages within him between his "diabolical love" of darkness and his "unearthly hate" for its effect on him. Marlow perceives that his own fascination with Kurtz is also a fascination with the same darkness that Kurtz has embraced, a "fascination of the abomination," which attracts every human heart. Marlow says of himself, "I had — for my sins, I suppose — to go through the ordeal of looking into it myself" (p. 82).

As Kurtz lies in the darkness on the steamer headed back downstream, he tells Marlow that he is dying. In the candlelight Marlow sees on his face "the expression of sombre pride, of ruthless power, of craven terror — of an intense and hopeless despair." Marlow wonders, "Did he live his life again in every detail of desire, temptation, and surrender during that supreme moment of complete knowledge? He cried in a whisper at some image, at some vision — he cried out twice, a cry that was no more than a breath: 'The horror! The horror!' " (p. 85).

In this novella written seventy years before America's large-scale involvement in Indochina, Conrad provides us with a prefiguration of the moral disintegration that would engulf U.S. troops in Vietnam. William Broyles, Jr., notes that for men war is the initiation into the power of life and death. "It is like lifting off the corner of the universe and looking at what's underneath. To see war is to see into the dark heart of things, that no-man's-land between life and death, or even beyond."[11] There are some forms of knowledge that, once attained, are irreversible. And the pain of such self-knowledge devours the soul. This is the testimony of countless Vietnam vets. The hero self-destructs. When the curtain fell on Vietnam, John Wayne was dead (figuratively speaking) and with him the ideal of masculine heroism as well as the hubris of America's civilizing mission in the world.

The Process of Moral Disintegration

Philip Caputo's combat memoir, *A Rumor of War*,[12] portrays as clearly as any narrative the gradual, step-by-step descent into the heart of darkness that American soldiers experienced in Vietnam. Caputo arrived in Danang, Vietnam, with the first unit of regular U.S. forces, a battalion of the Ninth Marine Expeditionary Brigade, on March 8, 1965. By the time he left Vietnam in June 1966, he was a seasoned warrior. After his discharge from the marines in 1967, he joined the *Chicago Tribune* as a war correspondent covering conflicts all over the world. This memoir, published eleven years after his tour of duty in Vietnam, bears the stamp of mature reflection on the nature of war in general and the unique characteristics of the Vietnam War, especially the process of moral deterioration that American soldiers experienced there.

A Rumor of War is a straightforward, three-part story that fits Arnold Van Gennep's typical rite of passage: separation (preparation for war); liminal rites (war experiences "in country"); and reincorporation back into "the world" after the tour of duty. It explores sequentially the loss of idealism and innocence, the descent into moral ambiguity and degradation, and finally the author's postwar attempt as a war correspondent to reconcile the fascination and the repulsion of war. Each chapter begins with an epigraph from narrators of other wars — Vegetius, a fourth-century Roman military writer; Shakespeare; Kipling; Hemingway; Thomas Hobbes; and especially Wilfred Owen and Siegfried Sassoon, whose works depict the senseless slaughter of World War I. These epigraphs not only give a hint of Caputo's thorough acquaintance with a vast body of war literature; they also imply that he has consciously crafted his memoir to answer the question, How was your war different from other wars?

Veterans from other wars have derided the Vietnam veterans for America's first loss. Vietnam veterans have responded in different ways: "We never lost a major battle"; "We were *not allowed* to win"; "The press and the antiwar movement undercut the national will to win"; or simply, "The war was fucked!" meaning that the goals were not clear and the military strategies selected were inappropriate for the type of war soldiers had to fight in Vietnam. Others have charged that by its very nature the war was unwinnable.

By comparing his war to previous wars, Caputo retraces the journey that called into question the entire American self-image. Even in the prologue we hear echoes of Conrad: "There was nothing familiar out where we were, no churches, no police, no laws, no newspapers, or any of the restraining influences without which the earth's population of virtuous people would be reduced by ninety-five percent. It was the dawn of creation in the Indochina bush, an ethical as well as a geographical wilderness. Out there, lacking restraints, sanctioned to kill, confronted by a hostile country and a relentless enemy, we sank into a brutish state" (p. xx). Caputo undergoes a change of consciousness that is more than a transition from innocence to maturity. It is a sober personal metamorphosis born of a confrontation with evil. To engage the reader in the author's personal journey, Caputo speaks with two voices. The first is Caputo the romantic warrior, responding to "the prince of Camelot," whose call — "Ask not what your country can do for you; ask what you can do for your country" — sent a generation of young men to Southeast Asia in search of the heroic. The second is Caputo the penitent, who catalogues the transformative experiences in a journey from romance to shame. Although the author does not specifically name stages in his descent into darkness, the careful reader can discern at least five such stages.

Stage 1
Discovery: The Enemy Is Human

The title of part 1 — "The Splendid Little War" — connotes the naïveté of fresh marines and their eagerness for battle. Caputo enlisted partly out of boredom and the desire to rebel against his parents, but mainly for heroic adventure. "I saw myself charging up some distant beachhead, like John Wayne in *Sands of Iwo Jima,* and then coming home a suntanned warrior with medals on my chest. . . . I needed to prove something — my courage, my toughness, my manhood. . . . *The Marine Corps Builds Men,* . . . and I became one of its construction projects" (pp. 6–7).

With this youthful exuberance and self-assurance the marines who landed in Danang in March 1965 were eager to do more than defend an airfield. They yearned to go on the offensive. "We had acquired the conviction that we could win this brushfire, and win it quickly, if we were only turned loose to fight. . . . We believed in our own publicity — Asian guerrillas did not stand a chance against U.S. marines. . . . There was nothing we could not do because we were Americans, and for the same reason, whatever we did was right" (p. 66).

In their first real combat encounter, a harrowing ninety-minute firefight, Caputo's company wound several Vietcong (VC). A manhunt ensues, following trails of blood through the tall grass. Rather than take a wounded man prisoner, a marine unsheathes his pistol and shoots him in the head, point blank. When they come upon a VC base camp that has been hastily abandoned and find letters and photographs of Vietnamese girlfriends and wives, Private First Class Lockhart turns to Caputo and says, "They're young men. They're just like us, Lieutenant" (p. 117). Caputo reflects on how this discovery of the humanity of the enemy disturbs them. Taught by the Marine Corps to kill the enemy and find pride in the killing, why then the dis-ease? His answer: "The drill fields and our first two months in Vietnam had dulled, but not deadened, our sensibilities. We retained a capacity for remorse and had not yet reached the stage of moral and emotional numbness" (p. 117). However, one of their number, rifleman Hanson, has already "passed beyond callousness into savagery." He is caught cutting an ear off the corpse of a VC.

Stage 2
Doubt: Getting Killed for Nothing?

The tone of the memoir changes dramatically when Caputo is assigned new responsibilities as regimental casualty reporting officer. Each day he must fill out casualty reports on both friendly and enemy troops, using euphemistic "militarese." Then he must record the numbers on the scoreboard that hangs on the wall behind Colonel Wheeler's desk. Because attrition is the declared strategy, body count and the kill ratio (proportion of enemy dead to one's own dead) have become supreme measures of success or failure.

Field commanders sense pressure to provide headquarters with high body counts and, consequently, are tempted to falsify numbers. Thus, whatever is left of a corpse is transported back to headquarters where Caputo has to match severed body parts and verify the count. As the fighting picks up in the fall of 1965, the corpses multiply. Since they cannot always be transported immediately, corpses are delivered in various stages of decomposition. When Caputo describes their appearance — "the mouths were opened wide, as if death had caught them in the middle of a scream" (p. 161) — the reader begins to sense the suppressed scream that is mounting within the regimental casualty reporting officer himself. Caputo has entered the anteroom of the lodging named abjection.

On one occasion four mangled VC bodies are brought in to headquarters. The colonel orders them placed on display until all the clerks get a look at them, "to get used to the sight of blood." The bodies lie on a trailer in the sun, and the odor increases as they decompose. Finally, when everyone has filed by, Caputo orders a driver to cart the bodies away for burial. No sooner have they been buried than Caputo is ordered to have the bodies dug up and brought back to headquarters because General Thompson from Military Assistance Command Vietnam is to visit regimental headquarters the next day, and Colonel Wheeler wants him to see the corpses. As if to mock this macabre display, Caputo returns to his desk and makes a cardboard plaque that he tacks to the front of his desk: "2LT. P. J. Caputo. Officer in Charge of the Dead."

The day after General Thompson's visit, Caputo sits down for his evening meal across from Chaplain Ryerson. The chaplain asks him about a marine who has been killed that day: "I just hope these boys are dying for a good reason, Lieutenant. What do you think? I just hope [they] aren't getting killed because some officer wants a promotion" (p. 168). Angered by the chaplain, Caputo tries to avoid the issue, but Ryerson is persistent: "Maybe you could explain what we're doing over here. You've been a platoon commander. When we got here, we were just supposed to defend the airfield for a while and then go back to Okinawa. Now we're in the war to stay and nobody has been able to explain to me what we're doing. I'm no tactician, but the way it looks to me, we send men out on an operation, they kill a few VC, or the VC kill them, and then pull out and the VC come right back in. So we're back where we started. That's the way it looks to me. I think these boys are getting killed for nothing" (p. 169). Caputo is rankled by the chaplain's morally superior attitude, but the conversation arouses his own dormant questions. "I still believed in the cause for which we were supposed to be fighting, but what kind of men were we, and what kind of army was it that made exhibitions of the human beings it had butchered?" (p. 170).

As the summer passes, Caputo records the names of more and more of his men who are being killed in action. One night he has a nightmare that gives new meaning to his title, officer in charge of the dead. In the nightmare he is given charge of a new platoon. They stand before him in the rain, three ranks deep: Devlin, with his face blown off; Lockhart; Bryce on one leg; Sullivan and Reasoner and all the others. " 'Platoon, rye-eet FACE! Sliiiing HARMS! For-WARD HARCH!' . . . They marched along, my platoon of crippled corpses. . . . I was proud of them, disciplined soldiers and beyond the end. They stayed in step even in death" (p. 189). Earlier in the book, after the first real battle, Caputo had declared: "We are learning to hate." Now, as commander of a platoon of the dead, hate is beginning to take control of him. Only this time it is turned inward as well. He despises himself, the scorekeeper.

Stage 3
From Doubt to Disillusionment

One night while Caputo is at his desk taking radio messages about those wounded and killed in action, word comes that Walter Neville Levy, one of his buddies from officer training school at Quantico, Virginia, has been killed. Caputo is devastated. Suddenly the full weight of a mean-

ingless war is upon him. "How do you tell parents that all
the years they had spent raising and educating their son
were for nothing? Wasted" (p. 209). Then for the first and
only time in the book Caputo uses the second person. He
addresses Levy, "whose ghost haunts me still": "You were
the first from our class of 1964 to die. There were others,
but you were the first and more: you embodied the best
that was in us.... You died for the man you were trying to
save, and you died *pro patria*" (p. 213).

Turning his attention to America, but still addressing
Levy, Caputo captures the sentiments of a generation of
soldiers: "You were faithful. Your country is not. As I write
this, eleven years after your death, the country for which
you died wishes to forget the war in which you died.
Its very name is a curse. There are no monuments to its
heroes, no statues in small-town squares and city parks, no
plaques, nor public wreaths, nor memorials.... It wishes to
forget and it has forgotten. But there are a few of us who do
remember.... We loved you for what you were and what
you stood for" (p. 213).

At this point the reader views this personal conversation between Caputo and his dead classmate as an interruption in the war narrative. This interruption is an indictment of American civilian failure after the war, namely
the unwelcome reception vets got upon their return to the
United States. Later in the memoir, however, when Caputo describes the proceedings of his own court-martial,
he indicts the military as well by exploring the repression,
denial, and insensitivity to the plight of the combat soldier
that were systemic within the chain of command during
the war.

Stage 4
The Price of Revenge: Guilt and Shame

By November 1965 Caputo has been the officer in charge
of the dead for over five months. Away from day-to-day
battles, with time to reflect on the sense of it all, he is af-

flicted with a virulent case of what the French call *le cafard*
but which Julia Kristeva sees as symptoms of abjection:
boredom, loss of energy, morbid depression, and hatred of
oneself and everything else. To escape *le cafard* Caputo requests reassignment to a combat unit. In one of the book's
classic passages he captures the moral absurdity of the war:
"According to those 'rules of engagement,' it was morally
right to shoot an unarmed Vietnamese who was running,
but wrong to shoot one who was standing or walking; . . . it
was wrong for infantrymen to destroy a village with white
phosphorus grenades, but right for a fighter pilot to drop
napalm on it. *Ethics seemed to be a matter of distance and
technology.* You could never go wrong if you killed people
at long range with sophisticated weapons. . . . In the patriotic fervor of the Kennedy years, we had asked, 'What can
we do for our country?' and our country answered, 'Kill
VC.' That was the strategy, the best our best military minds
could come up with: organized butchery. . . . [S]o who was
to speak of rules and ethics in a war that had none?"
(p. 218; emphasis added).

In such a moral wilderness, better to be back where
the action is than counting corpses and fearing insanity.
But there are other reasons for Caputo's attraction to combat. "The rights or wrongs of the war aside, there was
a magnetism about combat. You seemed to live more in-
tensely under fire" (p. 218). And then there was hatred,
"a hatred buried so deep that I could not then admit its
existence. . . . I burned with a hatred for the Viet Cong. . . . I
wanted a chance to kill somebody" (p. 219).

The chance to kill comes quickly. On January 5, the
battalion embarks on Operation Long Lance, the second
nocturnal helicopter assault in history, against a combined
force of the North Vietnamese Army and the VC. The
following day Charlie Company is ordered to search Ha
Na, a large village on the Vu Gia River about twenty-five
miles southwest of Danang. Caputo's platoon finds it a
hellish task to cut or blast their way through the thorny
hedgerows. They are caught in enemy crossfire as a ma-

jor battle erupts. "Then it happened. The platoon exploded. It was a collective emotional detonation of men who had been pushed to the extremity of endurance. I lost control of them and even of myself.... [W]e rampaged through the rest of the village, whooping like savages, torching thatch huts, tossing grenades into cement houses we could not burn" (p. 287). That night as they dig their foxholes, Caputo measures their feelings: "There was a sweetness in that inner quietude, but the feeling would not have been possible if the village had not been destroyed. It was as though the burning of Ha Na had arisen out of some emotional necessity. It had been a catharsis. We had relieved our own pain by inflicting it on others. But that sense of relief was inextricably mingled with guilt and shame" (pp. 288–89).

Stage 5
Confronting Evil in Oneself

About a month after Operation Long Lance, Caputo learns that two suspected VC are living in the nearby village of Giao-Tri. Haunted by all the losses his company is suffering from mines and booby traps in the neighboring region, Caputo wonders if these two are responsible for setting the traps. When two more of his men, "short-timers" with only four more days left on their tour of duty, are blown away, Caputo becomes obsessed with his own possible death and his desire to destroy the enemy. He instructs five of his men to kidnap the two suspects and bring them in for interrogation. Caputo the narrator remembers the order he gave to his men: "In my heart, I hoped Allen would find some excuse for killing them, and Allen read my heart. He smiled and I smiled back, and we both knew in that moment what was going to happen. There was a silent communication between us, an unspoken understanding: blood was to be shed" (p. 300).

When the deed is done, they discover that one of those killed was not a VC, but a friendly informant. A complaint is registered by the village chief with the South Vietnamese Army and then with the American military officials. Charges are brought against the squad members and against Caputo. His term in Vietnam is extended by four months so that sufficient time can be given to collect information for the trial.

At this point Caputo expands his moral reflection to embrace the corporate responsibility of the military and civilian chain of command. He recognizes his responsibility for these two killings, but he does not consider it murder. "Something evil had been in me that night. It was true that I had ordered the patrol to capture the two men if at all possible, but it was also true that I had wanted them dead.... I had transmitted my inner violence to the men. ... And yet, I could not conceive of the act as one of premeditated murder.... The thing we had done was a result of what the war had done to us" (p. 309).

War creates unusual stress: constant fear of snipers, ambushes, booby traps, mines, nighttime mortar attacks; inability to distinguish between hostile enemy soldiers and friendly or neutral civilians; daily pressure from superiors to kill the enemy and rewards for doing so. Surely these extenuating circumstances would soften the charge against Caputo. In a war with "free-fire zones" where civilians were regularly killed by bombs, artillery, and napalm, surely this killing would not be treated in a military court like a murder committed in Los Angeles in peacetime. "The deaths of Le Dung and Le Du could not be divorced from the nature and conduct of the war. They were an inevitable product of the war. America could not intervene in a people's war without killing some of the people" (p. 306). Surely the military court would understand the context in which these deaths occurred.

Caputo's hope is soon shattered. The military court cannot raise these issues, his legal counsel informs him, for to do so would be to admit the moral deterioration that occurs in war. "It could [not] even raise the question of the morality of American intervention in Vietnam" (p. 306).

For the military, the case is simple. If these five GIs and their officer are found guilty, then they could be charged with criminal behavior and the military itself exonerated. Every group has a few criminals, it could be claimed. On the other hand, if they are found innocent, then the military has given legal recourse to both parties, and justice has been served. No matter what the verdict, the military wins. Although not denying the culpability of the enlisted men and indeed his own role in issuing an order with evil intent, Caputo nevertheless concludes, "The war in general and U.S. military policies in particular were ultimately to blame for the deaths of Le Du and Le Dung. That was the truth and it was that truth which the whole proceeding was designed to conceal" (p. 313).

Having discovered that the guardians of Marine Corps honor — the judges of the military court — are unwilling or unable to confront moral ambiguity, Caputo finds the same blindness in his fellow officers. They cannot entertain the idea that either the enlisted men or Caputo could in any way be accused of homicide. "If the charges were proved, it would prove no one was guaranteed immunity against the moral bacteria spawned by the war. If such cruelty existed in ordinary men like us, then it logically existed in the others, and they would have to face the truth that they too harbored a capacity for evil. But no one wanted to make that recognition. No one wanted to confront his devil" (p. 313).

The neat solution for everyone would be a verdict of innocence. The military would avoid the moral ambiguities, the other officers and enlisted men would avoid recognizing their own demons, and those charged would be spared dishonor and punishment. The price for such a verdict would be the sacrifice of truth, truth about war, truth about America, truth about the military, and truth about individual human capacity for evil.

Assessment

Caputo's trial and the verdict of innocence lend credence to the claim that the two most significant taboos broken in Vietnam were the myth of American innocence and the myth of American power.[13] Breaking a taboo results in defilement. Rather than face the horror that accompanies defilement, the military court along with the rest of the chain of command preferred to maintain the myth of corporate innocence and national virtue. Rather than recognize limits to American power, they descended into ever-deeper levels of violence in an attempt to "exterminate the brutes" who were successfully challenging that power. Rather than revealing a redemptive violence, Vietnam revealed the true nature of our national "love affair with violence": a heart of darkness that dehumanizes those who embrace it.

Caputo himself did not descend to the depths of that darkness. He traveled downward toward the abyss and "went over to the dark side" when he lost control of his unit and they destroyed an entire village, but his encounter with that level of evil was only temporary. Vietnam did not alter his masculine ideal. He retained a fascination with war; after his tour in Vietnam he signed up as a war correspondent to cover wars in other parts of the world.

In the narrative, Caputo appears unaware of a fundamental internal contradiction: the impossibility of supporting the warriors without supporting the war they fight.[14] He directs his anger at his country for not making heroes of those who fought and died for it in a war that was produced by its moral blindness. His insight into the moral corruption of the military is classic, but that very insight serves to protect him personally from the abyss. Perhaps this is because his tour of duty was at the beginning of large-scale U.S. involvement, before widespread disillusionment set in among most American troops. To understand the more radical effects of the journey into the heart of darkness, we need to examine other narratives and interpret them in light of the experience of shame and abjection.

Chapter Four

Abjection

We're getting to be more like the savages we are up against.
> —Donald McQuinn, *Targets*

We destroyed ourselves over there, not the VC.
> —Charles Coleman, *Sergeant Back Again*

Upon each of our brains the war has lodged itself, a black crab feeding.
> —Gustav Hasford, *The Short-Timers*

A Terror-Filled Revelation:
Our Capacity for Evil

It was as if Sid had just been waiting for someone to record his story. "After I came back from Vietnam I shut down emotionally," he said. "Couldn't get close to women. I began therapy; in fact I tried every kind of therapy on the market — but nothing worked. In 1978 I saw the movie *Coming Home* and fell apart. Then I joined a rap group and began to mobilize my anger. Anger at how we were betrayed. For ten years I explored my anger. I'm Jewish, and as an adolescent I had been obsessed with the Nazis and angry that the Jews didn't fight back. The image I carried in my mind was of Nazis herding naked people into gas chambers with cattle prods. But anger wasn't all I had been repressing. In 1988 during a session of polarity therapy the therapist touched me under my scapula on the back, and I was flooded with guilt and shame, and the terrible recognition that I am like the Nazis. I had done my job, obeyed the orders, never questioned my superiors. In my job as army psychiatrist, I had sent men out to kill and maim. And they had slaughtered many innocent people. This was the secret knowledge buried within my unconscious for over twenty years, a secret knowledge churning within my soul, waiting to explode like an erupting volcano: I am no better than my own worst enemy! This is what I have to live with."

Although most of us would disagree with this moral analogy, we may accept one conclusion Sid has drawn: the revelation of his own *capacity* for evil destroys the Manichaean distinction between "us" and "them," the good guys and the bad guys. At the same time this revelation undermines the American self-understanding (the myth of innocent, righteous American power) that provided the rationale and the motivation for the Vietnam War.

Guilt and shame are inextricably mixed in Vietnam War narratives. In an interview, Bill Mahedy, vet chaplain and author, declared: "I've never met a combat vet who didn't feel guilt for those he killed in Vietnam." I realized only later that I should have asked him about shame as well. Our culture has been so influenced by psychologists like Sigmund Freud and anthropologists like Ruth Benedict that we have concentrated on guilt as a primary phenomenon and shame as a secondary one.

Social scientists often make a distinction between guilt cultures, where individuals are more "inner-directed," and shame cultures, where they are more "outer-directed." This view regards guilt as a feeling that results from the infraction of internalized codes, while shame results merely from flouting external social expectations. "Saving face," that special trait of Asian cultures (so it is said), is regarded as less profound than obeying one's conscience.

An examination of the dynamics of the descent into the heart of darkness points up the inadequacy of this understanding of guilt and shame and their relationship to each other. The disillusionment and disorientation that accompany this descent and that lead to the loss of identity are more closely associated with shame than with guilt. The feeling of guilt involves sins of commission. The appropriate remedy is confession, forgiveness, and restitution, even if the restitution must be made to someone other than the victim. Shame derives from sins of omission, especially a sense of failure. Sometimes it is failure to meet social expectations, but at the deepest level it is a failure to attain one's goals and live up to one's own self-image.

Helen Merrell Lynd's study of the relationship between shame and identity is particularly relevant to the experiences of Vietnam vets.[1] Lynd delineates several dimensions of shame. First, shame arises from experiences that uncover and expose intimate and vulnerable dimensions of the self. The exposure may be to others, but deeper and more painful is exposure to one's own eyes. In his novel *Body Count*,[2] William Turner Huggett provides one of the most graphic portraits of how the military uses the fear of shame to turn fresh officers into wise and tough leaders. Lieutenant Hawkins does fear external exposure (the loss of his men's confidence), but his greatest fear is the loss of self-respect that would result from failure to lead his men decisively, with courage and wisdom.

A second and deeper dimension of shame arises when one is exposed to parts of the self that have been hidden and repressed from consciousness. Such exposure upsets one's self-confidence, breeds self-doubt, shakes the foundations of selfhood. The military court and Philip Caputo's fellow officers could not even entertain questions about the moral context of the war, for such questions would expose them to frightening self-revelations. When the therapist touched the vet psychiatrist Sid on his scapula, Sid was flooded with an all-pervasive revelation of shame.

A third and still more basic level of shame derives from the exposure of misplaced confidence and trust in another person, group, ideology, or worldview. A vet chaplain explained his shame in this way: "My age group, . . . we were religious jingoists. We identified God and country. Question authority? Not us. That would be un-American and un-Christian. We thought we were Sir Galahads with the strength of ten because our hearts — our goals, our intentions, our ideals — were pure. We were being used by the government, and we didn't even know it. . . . God! How could we have been so stupid?" At this level shame is often mixed with rage directed toward the source of betrayal, whether it be a person, a group, or a system of beliefs. In chapter 5 when we examine the experiences of vets upon their return from Vietnam, we will see the prominence of this dimension of shame.

Finally, the deepest feeling of shame is that sense of abandonment that comes when one has nothing left to trust — no person, no group, no belief system, not even God. One vet expressed his rage at God for such abandonment: "God," he shouted, "you motherfucker! Where were you in Vietnam?"[3] This is true homelessness, when cynicism and skepticism slide on down into the pit of isolation and despair. "Loss of trust, exposure, failure, the feeling of homelessness — these experiences of shame — become still more unbearable if they lead to the feeling that there is no home for anyone, anywhere. . . . Experience of shame may call into question, not only one's own adequacy and the validity of the codes of one's immediate society, but the meaning of the universe itself."[4] The high rate of vet suicides and the fact that one-third of the nation's homeless are vets testify to the pervasiveness of this deepest legacy of shame.

The experience of deep shame leaves both individuals and groups with two alternatives, either denial of the revelation or the restructuring of identity in the light of what has been uncovered. Since the latter alternative requires a complete re-storying of one's life-narrative, most prefer to take the route of denial. After the war, America, like most of the vets, initially took the easier road. However, once we have lifted the corner of the universe — to use William Broyles's metaphor — and peered beneath, the images of what we have seen cannot be buried for long. They remain freeze-dried in the back of our eyes.

Abjection: A Portrait

Those who have the courage to embrace the revelation descend, personally or vicariously, into the heart of darkness. For those who have been most traumatized personally by the war, darkness takes the form of abjection. This is the term that Julia Kristeva uses to describe the *powers of horror* that have been unleashed in the twentieth century, the psychic and spiritual devastation that accompanies the violent collapse of meaning.[5] Abjection is a complex, multilayered reality, similar to the experience of shame. It has two magnetic poles, as it were, the fascinating and the repulsive, which are in constant interplay.

Societies order themselves by elaborating systems of meaning that distinguish between the clean and the unclean. At the physical level, pus, blood, vomit, urine, feces, corpses, and all else that symbolizes vulnerability or decay or death are unclean and repugnant. At the moral level, compromise, hypocrisy, deception, betrayal, and cruelty evoke a similar disgust. And yet the abject is not only repugnant; it is also and simultaneously attractive. "It beckons to us and ends up engulfing us."[6]

Abjection is brought into being by *jouissance* (the play of desire). *Jouissance* is a dangerous ecstasy, a transgressive pleasure that accompanies the breaking of taboos. "How do I explain — to my wife, my children, my friends — that I loved war as much as anything before or since?" asks William Broyles, Jr. "No sport I had ever played brought me to such deep awareness of my physical and emotional limits."[7] Abjection is thus a passion edged with the sublime. "One joys in it ... violently and painfully. ... So many victims of the abject are its fascinated victims — if not its submissive and willing ones."[8]

But victims they are, all the same, for abjection involves the awareness of corruption and sin; the breach of identity, system, and order; the loss of something that can never be recovered. "Abjection ... is immoral, sinister, scheming, and shady: a terror that dissembles, a hatred that smiles."[9]

As we shall see when we examine Gustav Hasford's novel *The Short-Timers,* laughter is frequently used to hold the horror at bay, but the laughter is never innocent. Kristeva writes, "If there is a gushing forth, it is neither jovial, nor trustful...[but] bare, anguished, and as fascinated as it is frightened."[10]

Abjection is produced by coming face-to-face with repugnant horror. Recall Morgan in *Fragments*. Just before dawn as the squad is hunkered down in holes on the side of a valley, Morgan has a dream. In the dream he and his unit are back in boot camp gagging on a horrible odor, the smell of death. Nothing they do — showers, washing clothes, scrubbing down the walls and floors — removes the smell. When he wakes up, there staring him in the face, not a foot away from his nose, is a rotting human skull cradled in an American helmet. Morgan bolts out of the hole screaming. If the enemy could penetrate their defenses — the claymore mines they had set up around the perimeter — and go undetected by lookouts with the latest night-vision technology while placing a rotting skull right next to a sleeping grunt, who could be safe anywhere? That is terror![11]

Abjection begins with a terrifying experience of defilement that produces repulsion, repugnance, and disgust; a skin-tingling loathing that causes fear, spasms, vomiting, retching, trembling. And yet it is at the same time a defilement that fascinates and attracts, a "spasm...as tempting as it is condemned. Unflaggingly, like an inescapable boomerang, a vortex of summons and repulsion places the one haunted by it literally beside himself."[12] Thus soldiers describe the "battle high" as "an ache as profound as the ache of orgasm."[13] Later reflection on the joy of killing produces guilt, remorse, and above all shame.

Sometimes Kristeva describes abjection as the experience of terror itself; at other times she portrays it as a product of terror, the overwhelming weight of meaninglessness that sucks life from the soul. This is an indication of the multifaceted nature of evil and our inability fully to denote the contours of this elusive mystery. In reality, the terror and the meaninglessness interact, each reinforcing the other. Terror produces revulsion and anger, which find expression in a vengeance fueled by fear, pride, and adrenaline; and that vengeance merges into bloodlust. Both the thrill of battle and the senseless killing in battle evoke guilt and shame. If one's gods are also destroyed in the process, as they were for American GIs in Vietnam, the soul is afflicted with a devouring, meaningless void, "a black crab feeding." Like the psychiatrist Sid, one reaches the nadir of darkness with the discovery that in the name of good, on behalf of the highest ideals, one has become the mirror image of evil itself, the embodiment of all the savagery one sought to destroy. "If it be true that the abject simultaneously beseeches and pulverizes the subject, one can understand that it is experienced at the peak of its strength when that subject, weary of fruitless attempts to identify with something on the outside, finds the impossible within; when it finds that the impossible constitutes its very *being*, that it *is* none other than abject."[14]

"The loss of innocence" is too tame a phrase to describe the mixture of depression and despair that comprises this massive weight of meaninglessness. The loss is much deeper. Some vets liken it to amputation, the violent severing of the soul itself, leaving only the nostalgic melancholy of a memory of wholeness forever lost.[15]

Two Examples of the Experience of Abjection in Vietnam

Loss of soul, the end result of living out the classic myths of American male identity, is the larger revelation of the Vietnam War. It has generated a body of absurdist literature and several quasi-nihilistic films. The novel to which we now turn has been classified in both categories; as we shall see, the classification misses the mark. Absurdist, yes. Nihilistic, no. Absurdist humor is deftly employed in protest against the annihilation implicit in the American narrative itself.

The Short-Timers

Philip Beidler observes that a number of novels published after 1975 have as their "obsessive center" the meanness that results from "a giving over of the soul to horror in warfare." This is meanness as in "rattlesnake mean, beaten-dog mean. It is the soul's ground zero, so to speak, the place one must go to...if one is even to begin talking significantly about a war where there was finally nothing to fight for save perhaps some animal sense of numb survival."[16] The meanness depicted here exposes that hidden darkness that can surface when national righteousness, wedded to the Enlightenment spirit of mastery and wielding the advanced weapons of science and technology, is frustrated. It is also an ironic illustration of "friendly fire," how the escalation of meaningless violence turns back upon the perpetrator in a pattern of self-inflicted dehumanization. Gustav Hasford's *The Short-Timers* is representative of the absurdist genre of war stories, which combine horror with humor to portray war as grotesque irony.[17]

Unlike more realistic novels that move gradually from innocent naïveté to violent disillusionment, Hasford's book uses the comic voice to paint a portrait of the war that is, from beginning to end, a sustained crescendo of callous brutality, "a spare but minutely rendered poetics of evil."[18] Hasford depicts how American grunts, trapped in a meaningless struggle for survival, are reduced to bravado and gallows humor to protect themselves from the horror in which they are enmeshed, as if the meaner and tougher and more callous a person becomes the greater the chance of survival in combat. The careful reader is able to discern a spiraling descent deeper and deeper into evil, even in the midst of what appears on the surface as unrelieved sick humor. As an epigraph for the central portion of the narrative, Hasford borrows a line from William S. Burroughs: "A psychotic is a guy who's just found out what's going on" (p. 29). The first part of the narrative (marine boot camp at Parris Island) implies that a recruit has only two choices, either to become a hardened killer or to go mad, and the remainder of the narrative illustrates how gallows humor becomes the killer's primary defense against finding out what's going on.

Nonetheless, this defense is not strong enough to protect everyone. The central portion of the narrative, entitled "Body Count," takes place in Vietnam during ten days of the crucial 1968 Tet Offensive launched by the VC (Vietcong) and the NVA (North Vietnamese Army). The first epigraph for this section is from Allen Ginsberg's poem *Howl:* "I saw the best minds of my generation destroyed by madness, starving hysterical naked..." "Body Count" describes the journey into madness taken by several GIs.

Joker, the narrator, has become a cynical and hardened combat journalist responsible for training a new photographer, Rafter Man, so named because he fell out of the rafters at the Thunderbird Club one night while drunk and trying to get a closer look at the belly dancers on stage. By recounting the experiences that turn Rafter Man into a killer and Joker into a combat team commander, Hasford focuses the story like the lens of a microscope, gradually but relentlessly zeroing in on the face of evil.

One day back at headquarters when Joker and Rafter Man run into Cowboy, Joker's best friend from boot camp, Rafter man gets a dose of the "I'm meaner than you" braggadocio that grunts use to taunt one another. After introducing the members of the Lusthog Squad including Crazy Earl, T.H.E. Rock, and Animal Mother (who wears a necklace of Vietcong ears), Cowboy declares that they are "the baddest of the bad, the leanest of the lean, the meanest of the mean....Man, we are life takers and heartbreakers" (p. 34). Later in the heat of battle we learn of the competition among squad members for a higher "confirmed kill" rate.

Terry Frazier recounts how men take pride in killing, even glory in it as a form of self-aggrandizement. "Soldiers don't feel squeamish about killing. If you set up an ambush and some enemy soldier gets through, you get angry at yourself and your squad for being lousy shots. If you do get them, you search with animation for weapons (they don't always have them), and then, in many cases you go calmly through the process of body mutilation (each unit has its style) — just as part of the job. It seems perfectly justified because 'they do it.' "[19]

One night the men in their *hootch* are bored and decide to "barbecue" some "Vietcong" rats. They place bits of chocolate in a box in the corner and wait for the rats to gather. Then they turn on the lights, squirt lighter fluid into the box, and light it. "Rats explode from beneath the board like shrapnel from a rodent grenade" (p. 58). After chasing down and killing the flaming creatures, they do a body count and compare their kill ratio with that of the platoon next door. Mr. Payback breaks off the tail of a rat, swallows it, and says, "Ummm...love them crispy critters." Grinning, he picks up another rat and hands it to Rafter Man, who freezes. "What's wrong, New Guy?" says Mr. Payback. "Don't you want to be a killer?" (p. 59). A few hours later, when Winslow has been mangled by the direct hit of a mortar, Rafter Man holds in his hand a bloody chunk of Winslow's flesh. With a cold, sardonic smirk on his face and looking directly at Mr. Payback, Rafter Man places the flesh on his tongue, grits his teeth, closes his eyes, and swallows.

Having proved that he wants to become a killer, Rafter Man is eager to "get into the shit." Captain January obliges by ordering Joker and Rafter Man to the besieged city of Hue, the ancient, sacred imperial capital. With Walter Cronkite due the next day, the captain needs photographs of Vietcong atrocities. "Get me photographs of indigenous civilian personnel who have been executed with their hands tied behind their backs, people buried alive, priests with their throats cut, dead babies.... Don't *even* photograph any naked bodies unless they're mutilated" (p. 51).

Joker and Rafter Man gather their equipment and weapons and hitch a ride up Highway 1 on the front of a tank whose name is painted on the barrel: *BLACK DRAGON: we exterminate household pests.* When they enter the ancient city, they find Cowboy and his Lusthog Squad resting in the ruins of a house, holding a mock celebration with "Tiger Piss" (Vietnamese beer). Cowboy is passing out stacks of money (Vietnamese piasters) he has looted from nearby mansions. Seated next to Crazy Earl is the "guest of honor," an NVA corporal with a pile of money in his lap, a can of beer in his hand, and his split lips curled back in a death grin. "I made him sleep," says Crazy Earl, putting his arm around the corporal's shoulders. Then he puts his forefinger to his lips and whispers, "Shhh. He's resting now" (p. 75). Before returning to battle, another grunt named Alice cuts off the corporal's feet and throws them into his blue canvas shopping bag with the other feet he has cut off Vietcong corpses.

In the assault on the Citadel, an explosion knocks Joker out. When Joker awakens, Cowboy explains that a machine gun cut down Crazy Earl when he went berserk and tried to "do a John Wayne"; that a sniper wounded several men in a graveyard, pinning down everyone who tried to rescue them and then slowly blowing away the wounded men's appendages one at a time; that the platoon commander, Mr. Shortround, was fragged (killed by a fragment grenade) by Animal Mother because he would not let them rush the sniper. The platoon regroups to attack from the rear. When Rafter Man succeeds in wounding the sniper, they discover that she is less than five feet tall and no more than fifteen years old. Rafter Man is ecstatic. "Look at her!" he exclaims as he struts around the moaning girl, whose guts are spilling out of bullet holes. "Look at her! Am I bad? Am I a menace? Am I a life *taker*? Am I a heart*breaker*?" (p. 100). As they prepare to move on, Joker protests that they can't just leave the dying girl. No one wants to shoot her point blank, so Joker reluctantly delivers the coup de grace. There is silence, then Alice says, "Man, you are one hard dude. How come you ain't a grunt?"

Animal Mother, who has had frequent confrontations with Joker because Joker refuses to be intimidated by him, fears that he is losing status. Thus, Animal Mother chops off the girl's head and sticks it in everyone's face saying, "Hard? *Now* who's hard? Now who's hard, mother-fuckers?" Rafter Man wonders if Joker wants credit for the kill. "I shot her first, Joker. . . . That's one confirmed for me." He collects her rifle belt and Simarov carbine; Alice "souvenirs" her feet and her gold ring; and Rafter Man poses for photographs with his foot on the mutilated remains. As they move out, Rafter Man sees his reflection in a shattered window. He stops and stares for a long time at the new smile upon his face. It is a moment of revelation. He has become a killer. Perhaps he remembers Joker's earlier remark: "[W]hat you do, you become" (p. 46). Then he drops the carbine and the rifle belt and stumbles off down the road in a daze. Later, traumatized by what he has become, Rafter Man will not take even elementary precautions. He will be run over accidentally by an American tank.

The climax of the narrative takes place at Khe Sanh, to the northwest of Hue, where American troops are pinned down and surrounded by the NVA. They fear a repeat of the devastating defeat of the French in 1954 in a similar valley, Dien Bien Phu. A colonel has transferred Joker from the press corps to the Lusthog Squad out of pique, because Joker was wearing an antiwar peace symbol and forgot to salute. Each day the squad goes out on a search-and-destroy mission, trying to keep the enemy from amassing troops too close to their perimeter. On one outing New Guy has joined the squad (he won't get a name until some defining event occurs), and Animal Mother is explaining why the other squad members despise him. "These guys will tell you that I am a monster, but I'm the only grunt in this squad that doesn't have his head up his ass. In this world of shit, monsters survive." Then he recognizes that killing is more than meanness in service of survival. It can also be an exhilarating power-trip. "If you kill for fun, you're a sadist. If you kill for money, you're a mercenary. If you kill for both, you're a Marine" (p. 136).

As the squad penetrates deeper and deeper into the forest, a shot rings out. Alice, the point man, is down. When Doc Jay, the corpsman, runs forward to assist Alice, he too is wounded. It's a jungle version of the city scene in Hue: a sniper lames the point man without killing him, knowing that marines never leave their wounded unattended. Then everyone who comes to the rescue is also wounded and slowly executed, body part by body part. Knowing this, Cowboy, the squad leader, orders everyone down. New Guy is too enraged to obey and lunges ahead firing blindly. When he reaches Alice and Doc Jay, he too is shot.

Cowboy then orders the others to retreat, but Animal Mother reminds him, "Marines never abandon their dead or wounded, Mr. Squad Leader, *Sir*" (p. 148). Realizing that he is trapped, Cowboy turns command over to Joker, takes a pistol, and moves out toward his wounded men. At that moment they are surprised by the sound of laughter. After a moment Joker understands that only a sniper who does not fear death would risk revealing his position by laughing. He too laughs, a duet of dark humor. "Sooner or later the squad will be laughing too," Joker thinks to himself. "Soon they won't be afraid. The dark side will surface and they'll be like me; they'll be Marines." Then he adds, as if defining "marine" as a state of awareness, as an all-pervasive awareness of death, "once a Marine, always a Marine" (p. 151).

When Cowboy reaches the wounded men, the sniper again finds his range, hitting Cowboy in the right leg, then the left, then the crotch. Before his upper body is hit, Cowboy quickly shoots each of his men in the head and then raises the pistol to his own temple. A shot rings out! The pistol drops and Cowboy looks first at the hole the sniper has put in his hand, then helplessly back at Joker. Animal Mother is wild with rage. He steps forward saying, "We'll

go for Cowboy, give the sniper too many targets. ... " Joker
steps in front of him, and Animal Mother threatens to cut
him in half. Joker turns his back on Animal Mother, fully
expecting to die. Then he raises his gun and shoots Cowboy through the left eye. Joker narrates: "Silence. Animal
Mother lowers his M-60 [machine gun]. ... Everyone re-
laxes. Everyone hates my guts, but they know I'm right. I
am their sergeant; they are my men. Cowboy was killed by
sniper fire, they'll say, but they'll never see me again; I'll be
invisible" (pp. 152–53).

Joker orders his men to saddle up. As they prepare
to leave, he studies their faces and sees their need to regain emotional control. Stifling his own grief at having
to kill his best friend, Joker relies on the only defense he
has in the face of massive evil. "Man-oh-man," he says,
"Cowboy looks like a bag of leftovers from a V.F.W. barbecue. Of course, I've got nothing against dead people. Why,
some of my best friends are dead!" (p. 153). The irony
of war, Hasford tells us, is that "short-timers" have become "Kurtz-timers" (*kurtz* = "short," in German), those
who have been marked for all time with the spirit of darkness embodied by Kurtz. Even though every grunt dreams
of the day when he will board the "Freedom Bird" and
fly back to "the land of the big PX," there is no escape
from the haunting awareness of evil that has imprisoned
his soul. "Those of us who survive to be short-timers will
fly the Great Speckled Bird back to hometown America.
But home won't be there anymore and we won't be there
either. Upon each of our brains the war has lodged itself, a
black crab feeding" (p. 151).

Hasford stirs the imagination to ponder diverse issues.
Duty: how Cowboy, like countless other GIs, does his duty
while knowing he will die; how Animal Mother, no matter
how much the war has dehumanized him, still possesses
human qualities of honor and loyalty and will not abandon a wounded buddy. Toughness: how Joker avoids going
over the edge into uncontrolled violence; how toughness

allows him to shoot his best friend and still use humor for survival, even though it is tearing his heart out; how in the end toughness eludes Animal Mother — he, after all, was ready to rush the sniper and get everyone killed; how Rafter Man wasn't tough enough to survive his self-image as killer. Revenge: how "payback" is a powerful motive inextricably linked to our passion for justice, yet is so likely to drive a person over the edge into an all-consuming darkness; how bloodlust serves both survival and self-aggrandizement; how Alice fears no evil because of the knowledge that he is evil. And finally, self-knowledge: how, like a boomerang, violence turns back upon the violent one; how, like friendly fire, the conscious or even unconscious knowledge that I have become for others the Grim Reaper, and harbor the same capacity for evil as my own worst enemy, plunges me into a self-annihilating darkness.

Hasford takes us a step beyond Caputo, to the very depths of the abyss, to the most profound apocalypse that Vietnam veterans have to share with America: a revelation of the consequences of our capacity for evil, consequences that flow logically from the dangerous myths of innocence, goodness, and benevolent power embodied in the narratives of our national identity. "We didn't know who we were until we got [to Vietnam]. We thought we were something else."[20] Even though much of America would like to deny or repress this revelation, it is now lodged in our minds, like a black crab feeding.

Apocalypse Now

The second illustration of the experience of abjection is found in Francis Coppola's 1979 film, *Apocalypse Now*. This film uncovers the dehumanizing and self-destructive character of our nation's mission in Vietnam. Whereas many novelists make passing reference to Conrad's work, Coppola interprets the Vietnam War as America's modern version of *Heart of Darkness*.

Colonel Walter E. Kurtz of the Green Berets has crossed over into Cambodia with a band of Montagnard soldiers. From there he carries out his own war against the Vietcong, the North Vietnamese, and the Cambodians. Like Conrad's Kurtz, he too has "kicked himself loose" from control by higher military authority, terrifying his enemies and using "unsound methods" to assassinate South Vietnamese whom he suspects are double agents. The American military has tried to rein him in, to no avail. He has become an outlaw, wanted for murder.

Captain Willard, the Marlow figure, also works for "the Company" (CIA) as a "hit man" with six "kills" under his belt. He is sent into Cambodia on a patrol boat to "terminate" Kurtz. John Hellmann, the most perceptive of the critics of the movie, notes elements of both the frontier western and the hard-boiled detective story in *Apocalypse Now*.[21] Kurtz embodies all the qualities and values of the American mythic hero, a Green Beret called to the frontier to enter the wilderness and claim it for civilization. He is intelligent, brave, tough, uninterested in personal gain, totally dedicated to his cause, brutal when necessary, but very protective of his own troops. In Vietnam, however, violence leads not to regeneration and hero status but only to greater violence, until the hero is transmogrified into a mad, blood-lusting savage. In this regard Kurtz is representative of the media's image of the American GI in Vietnam.

Willard, in contrast, represents the hard-boiled detective, a twentieth-century descendant of the western hero but sophisticated, cynical, and almost mad himself. Elements of the hard-boiled detective plot include: (1) the journey of the detective hero in search of a grail — in this case, Kurtz (America's lost mission, gone mad in the Cambodian jungle); (2) encounters with obstacles that reveal ignorance, incompetence, and malevolence in society itself, often in the form of corrupt officers of the law — in this case, the inanities and atrocities of the American military; (3) the apprehension of the criminal, which restores the moral ideals of society, in spite of the corruption of society. In *Apocalypse Now* this third element is altered because in "terminating" Kurtz, Willard symbolically destroys the American myth of special virtue and special mission.

The film opens with Willard lying semiconscious on a bed in a cheap Saigon hotel, dreaming of helicopters flying over forests ablaze with napalm. We hear the acid-rock song "This Is the End" by the Doors. On the table is an almost-empty glass of whiskey and a revolver. When an actual helicopter outside Willard's window awakens him, we learn by voiceover that the war has destroyed his marriage and that he has returned to Vietnam in search of a mission. Noting that every minute he stays in the hotel he gets weaker and "Charlie" gets stronger, Willard gets up to practice kung fu. Seeing his image in the mirror, he smashes it (symbolizing a self-destructive urge), chugalugs the entire bottle of whiskey, and sinks onto the floor crying and holding his blood-soaked hand. When two soldiers enter his room and ask his name, he responds, "What are the charges?" believing that they have come to arrest him for his own illegal but officially commissioned assassinations.

The soldiers take Willard to headquarters where a general and several other intelligence officers tell him about Kurtz, who has "taken the law into his own hands," apparently oblivious to the fact that in their own intelligence gathering they also are a law unto themselves. They assign him a seventh illegal assassination: to "terminate" Kurtz. With characteristic irony they play a tape of Kurtz's voice but do not appear to understand when Kurtz says, "What do you call it when the assassins accuse the assassin?" As Willard is dismissed, one officer underscores the secrecy of the mission: "This mission does not exist, nor will it ever exist." When Willard tells us, "There is no way to tell [Kurtz's] story without telling my own, and if his story is a confession, then so is mine," we have a hint that Willard is Kurtz's double; in killing Kurtz, he will also be killing that image of himself that embodies the mythic American hero.

On the way up the Mekong River, our detective hero

has four experiences that correspond to obstacles the traditional hero must overcome. In Willard's case they are not so much obstacles as illustrations of the insanity of the war. For example, at a large Vietcong village a unit of the air cavalry, led by "Big Duke" Kilgore, a latter-day General Patton whose helicopter gunships swoop in playing Wagner's "The Ride of the Valkyries," is reenacting a massacre of the "Indians" merely to make that part of the river safe for surfing on the six-foot swells. Watching fire roast every creature in the village, swaggering "Big Duke" declares his love for "the smell of victory" (napalm) and expresses regret that "some day this war's gonna end."

Colonel Kurtz's camp, the crumbling ruins of an ancient Buddhist temple, is even more barbaric than the Inner Station in *Heart of Darkness*. Not only decapitated heads but entire bodies hang from trees and posts in the yard where sacrifices are offered by the armed Montagnards to the godlike colonel. Leaving "Chef" on the boat with instructions to call in an air strike if he does not return by 2200 hours, Willard goes in search of the dying Colonel Kurtz. He is captured instead, placed in a bamboo "tiger cage," and terrorized by Kurtz, who drops the decapitated head of Chef in his lap. When Kurtz releases him, Willard realizes it is because Kurtz wants help both in dying and in interpreting to the outside world the apocalypse he has experienced.

Coppola provides apparent parallels to Conrad's account of self-annihilation resulting from an embrace of the darkness, but sometimes with a shift of emphasis. In *Heart of Darkness* it is Marlow who observes that Kurtz is hollow. In *Apocalypse Now* Willard listens as Kurtz himself reads T. S. Eliot's "The Hollow Men," which was inspired by Conrad's work. At the end of the manuscript that Colonel Kurtz has written, Willard finds the words, "Drop the Bomb. Exterminate them all." This is a projection of Kurtz's own desire to die, but it also reminds us of a similar violent streak in those who favored bombing North Vietnam "back into the Stone Age." "You have a right to kill me but not to call me a murderer," Kurtz tells Willard. "You have no right to judge me." This brings to mind not only Marlow's warning to his companions but also the hypocritical reception that awaited Vietnam veterans upon their return to "the world."

Most revealing is the colonel's attempt to justify his excesses. "It is impossible to describe what is necessary to those who do not know what horror is," he tells Willard. "Horror and moral terror are your friends, or they are your enemies." Then he describes how he came to embrace horror and commit unspeakable acts without regret. As a Green Beret involved in health care for the villagers, he inoculated children in one camp, only to learn later that the Vietcong had cut off every vaccinated arm. "The genius of that, the will to do that! Men who are moral and at the same time are able to use their primordial instincts to kill without feeling, without passion, without judgment. Because it is judgment that defeats us." The irony of course is that Kurtz thought he could give free rein to his "primordial instincts" without self-judgment. He too is dying from self-inflicted moral pain. When Willard kills him with a machete, he is merely completing the process that Kurtz himself has begun by embracing the darkness of his murderous "primordial instincts."

We have noted before that there is little difference, morally, between Kurtz and Willard, and indeed the entire American military operation in Vietnam. When Kurtz asks Willard, "Are you an assassin?" Willard replies, "I am a soldier," but he knows that assassins have sent him on his seventh mission and that in Vietnam the line between soldiering and assassination is very thin. Upon receiving his mission to "terminate" Kurtz, Willard reflects to himself: "Charging a man with murder in this place is like handing out speeding tickets at the Indy 500." After observing the massacre by "Big Duke" Kilgore's air cavalry, he comments on the voiceover: "If that's how Kilgore fought the war, I began to wonder what they really had against Kurtz.

It wasn't just insanity and murder. There was enough of that to go around for everyone."

Willard also knows that "[Kurtz's] story is my story." Coppola provides ample clues that Willard is Kurtz's double; like Kurtz, Willard kills without feeling, passion, or judgment; and like Kurtz, Willard too lacks "any decent restraint." Thus, notes Hellmann, "The ritualized assassination, with its psychologically resonant images of Willard rising from the river, entering a long corridor, and meeting a similarly painted Kurtz face-to-face, ... suggests that [Willard] is in fact killing not an external evil, but his unconscious self."[22] Since Kurtz and Willard both represent embodiments of the American mythic hero, the ritual murder symbolizes the necessary death of the American myth of special virtue and special mission. As he prepares to kill Kurtz, Willard tells us, "They were going to make me a major for this, and I wasn't even in their fucking army anymore," indicating his break with the past. Afterward he refuses to take Kurtz's place in the cult of death. When the patrol boat is once again heading downstream and the radio requests coordinates for an air strike, Willard turns it off. The rain washes the paint from his face, symbolizing an end to the myth and the violence that it occasions.

Conclusion

The revelation of our own capacity for evil is filled with terror, a terror that is at once attractive and repulsive. With time this new knowledge acts like a millstone around the neck, pulling a person into greater violence in a futile attempt to deny this knowledge and, at the same time, dragging that person into greater despair. The result is the experience of abjection, a form of defilement so repulsive that no single term is adequate to describe it. Disillusionment, disorientation, isolation, alienation, homelessness — all these are involved. But above all, it is experienced as loss of soul, the disappearance of all *élan vital*.

Chapter Five

Coming Home
to a God That Failed

All the vets I know are POWs, still in some way imprisoned by the war. Some of them are also MIAs, Missing in America.
> —Comment by a student, the spouse of a vet

There is no God for me after Vietnam.
> —Ron Kovic

A psychotic is a guy who's just found out what's going on.
> —Gustav Hasford, *The Short-Timers*

What Was "Wasted" in Vietnam?

The class assignment that evening was a two-page reflection paper on the warrior's experience of returning home. The weekly reading material included first-person accounts by vets of their homecoming. The stories described how they had been spat upon and taunted as "baby-killers" by vicious and self-righteous antiwar activists; how they were shunned by friends and misunderstood by family. After a discussion of the readings I asked if anyone wanted to share his or her assigned paper with the class. An uneasy silence followed, reflecting our sense of shame. Then a vet on the left side of the room cleared his throat and began to read in a hushed voice. "It didn't take long to realize that I was a casualty of war. My coun-

105

try did not want me, was embarrassed by me. No one cared what had happened to me; no one wanted to listen to the horrors of war. My country sent me to do evil and then hid from me because I reminded them of it. I was a victim of America's arrogance, and I was being blamed for it."

Vets differ in their assessment of the war — its purpose, the strategies, the lessons learned, even the outcome — but on one thing they are unanimous: upon their return home they all experienced betrayal and abandonment by a large segment of the American people. Defeated for the first time in its history, the nation wanted a scapegoat. So the vets were attacked by all sides. The doves blamed them for fighting, the hawks maligned them for losing. Every vet I have interviewed harbors deep resentment. Every piece of literature produced by Vietnam vet organizations echoes a note of flagrant injustice. Robert Bly, guru of the men's movement that flourished in the 1980s, believes that the deepest wound that the men of the Vietnam Generation suffered was betrayal of the young by the old. When fathers lie to sons, the sons' world falls apart.[1] The major task for vets, says marine veteran Rev. Michael Stuart, is not their need to reconcile with the Vietnamese against whom they fought, but "the need to reconcile with the American people in their midst, a much greater challenge. For many Vietnam veterans feel that they have no good reason to trust anyone here again and cannot find within themselves the ability to forgive. For more than two decades, Vietnam veterans have been maligned, scorned, shunned and ignored here in the U.S. and up until *now* their varied reflections of war experiences have been of little interest to the American public."[2]

War is always a disillusioning experience for the combat soldier, but if the cause for which one fights appears just and the warrior receives a hero's welcome at home, the deepest revelations are usually repressed and ignored. Even if individual soldiers are profoundly changed, their inner experience of darkness is not shared with society because it would contradict the public version of war and diminish their self-esteem, to say nothing of their status as heroes. Paul Fussell, a leading interpreter of the literature of twentieth-century wars, believes that this is exactly what happened to Americans after World War II. The horror was suppressed amid euphemistic censorship and heroic accolades piled on returning soldiers. "Thus, as experience, the suffering was wasted."[3] Nothing was learned about human nature, the descent into darkness, or the consequences of projecting one's own capacity for evil onto the enemy. In fact World War II strengthened the mythic landscape of American political messianism, setting the stage for the cold war and a self-righteous crusade between two equally Manichaean ideologies in Southeast Asia a decade and a half later.

The contrast between the soldiers' return from World War II and from Vietnam could hardly have been greater. Whereas the former returned en masse and in glory — ticker-tape parades, honorific speeches, keys to the city, job offers, a generous GI bill — the latter returned alone, one by one, in ignominy. Not only did they bear the brunt of tragic political and military miscalculations by American authorities; they also bore witness in their flesh to the demise of fundamental elements of the American narrative. The vets are certainly justified in their rage. They are victims of betrayal not only by presidents, generals, and the nation at large but also by cultural myths. They paid the price for the naïveté and the hubris — the "evil imaginations of the heart"[4] — embedded in our national story. In this regard they were "wounded for our transgressions, crushed for our iniquities."

Does this mean that their experience has been wasted? The GIs in Vietnam gave new meaning to the word "wasted." In combat, soldiers use euphemisms to soften the experience of killing and dying. But "he was wasted" is not as neutral as "he bought the farm." "Wasted" connotes cynicism, senseless death, needless destruction. Many vets feel not only that the war was senseless but also that their lives have been needlessly destroyed because of the way

they were treated when they returned home. My question
is: What were the alternatives?

Could they have received a hero's welcome, given all
they had learned about the destructiveness of the John
Wayne myth that sent many of them to Vietnam in the
first place? They did risk their lives in service of country and suffered the loss of limb and soul. And yes, they
summoned the courage to face the fear of death and
still perform their duties under fire. Many medals were
awarded for acts of unusual bravery. But the war itself was
too wrong for its warriors to be welcomed home as heroes.
In the classical doctrine of the just war, certain questions
are raised about *jus ad bellum* (the justice *of* a war) and
different questions about *jus in bello* (just methods for fighting *in* a war). During Desert Storm we heard the slogan,
"Support the warriors even if you don't support the war."
But this is morally impossible, for *jus ad bellum* cannot be
separated from *jus in bello*. Soldiers sent to fight a war
will interpret any opposition to that war as an act that
weakens their morale and demeans their sacrifices. Vietnam vets themselves recognize intuitively the moral unity
of the ends for which a war is fought and the means used
to fight it. Those who threw their medals onto the steps
of the Capitol in Washington during the April 1971 protest
against the war realized that they could not be proud of
having fought in an evil war, no matter how heroic their
individual acts of courage.

Another alternative — in fact from an ethical standpoint the only appropriate type of homecoming — would
have been bipartisan governmental admission of error,
public confession by top-ranking government and military
officials, and a request that the vets forgive the nation
for sending them to fight in what the grunts themselves
described as "a war that was fucked." No American administration, Democrat or Republican, hawkish or dovish,
could face such an admission and the criminal charges
that would have emerged from it. Nor were the American
people able to face the deeper meaning of the revelations

that emanated from the war. What was "wasted" in Vietnam was the continuity of the American story. To face the demise of the American national identity was too painful then, and for most it is still too painful now.

To return to our original question: Does this mean that the sacrifices of American vets were "wasted"? I think not. William Searle, a vet turned professor of literature, notes that American disenchantment with the war "caused many soldiers to confront the implications of their own acts."[5]

I read this comment to mean that *because* they received such a hostile reception at home, vets could not bury the past or lose sight of the revelation they had received. They alone had entered into the heart of darkness, and they alone were in position to interpret its meaning to the rest of us. Like Oedipus, they suffer not only from what they did but even more from the *knowledge* of what they did,[6] a knowledge forced upon them by the reception they received back home.

While they were in Vietnam, combat soldiers *experienced* the descent into darkness and the resulting powers of horror, but few *understood* their experience until they returned home. Understanding requires a period of gestation during which experience is weighed and sifted. While in Vietnam, GIs were busy just staying alive and controlling their emotions. An old U.S. *Officer's Guide* describes the struggle with oneself that soldiers undergo in battle: "Physical courage is little more than the ability to control the physical fear which all normal men have, and cowardice does not consist in being afraid but in giving way to fear."[7] Emotional distancing and psychic numbing are necessary techniques for survival, and when these failed, soldiers in Vietnam turned to alcohol and other drugs to avoid reflecting on their experiences. One vet reports: "The worst thing that happened to me ... [was that] I learned to see the Vietnamese as people.... From that point on, I had to be stoned."[8]

Had America won the war or even succeeded in staving off ignominious defeat, the warriors' homecoming would have been different. Fewer vets would suffer from post–traumatic stress disorder, imprisonment, and homelessness. Fewer would have committed suicide. But little would have been learned for future generations because combat vets would not have been forced to make sense of defeat or confront the nation with the dark dimensions of its shadow. The American narrative would have survived intact to haunt another generation of young men and women. The tragedy is that the price of collective change is so high and that one group of people carries the burden of historical redirection for the whole nation. Again the prophet Isaiah provides the clue: "Upon [them] was the punishment that [may make] us whole; and by [their] bruises we [may be] healed."

I use the subjunctive mood here because there is no guarantee that the nation will heed the revelation of its vicarious victims. Nonetheless, the American narrative will never be the same. "We brought home an infection," says one vet in a therapy group. "It'll be around for a long time."[9] A new consciousness has emerged as a result of the vets' intense moral struggle — a genuinely heroic struggle — to survive and reinterpret the meaning of America. Now we all face the hermeneutical crisis that arises from the "collision of narratives."[10] *Their* new experience can no longer be interpreted in terms of *our* old narrative. Thus, the tables are turned. *Their* healing now requires *our* wounding and our joint cooperation in revising the American story.

A God That Failed

Now let us examine in greater detail the various elements of the traditional American story to understand the nature of the loss. Earlier we referred to Viktor Frankl, founder of logotherapy, who believed the central human need, more basic than the drive for pleasure or power, is the will to meaning, the need to situate our lives in the context of a pattern and a purpose that make sense of our experience and of the world around us. The intensity of this need varies from individual to individual and is more acutely felt in times of crisis when a society's pattern of life is under threat. If the crisis is severe enough and long enough, personal and social identity is undermined.

American GIs first went to Vietnam inspired by New Frontier images of adventure, sacrifice, heroism, service — the virtuous ideals of American western expansion. They would preserve a small, fledgling nation from the evils of international communism and assist a backward people to achieve the blessings of political freedom and economic abundance. In the process they would bring honor to themselves and their country. Letters that the first GIs sent to family and friends back home document their expectation of a quick victory over a weak and disorganized enemy.

As the months turned into years, with no victory in sight despite the massive infusion of over half a million U.S. troops, and as the level of senseless violence increased, the war gradually lost all meaning. Instead of expecting an early victory, GIs were reduced to the single goal of survival and escape from the war. Many narratives recount the soldiers' discovery that instead of helping the South Vietnamese, Americans had themselves become the enemy of those they came to rescue.

A celebrated passage from Tim O'Brien's novel *Going after Cacciato* captures the American GIs' confusion better than any other single passage from the literature:

> They did not know even the simple things: A sense of victory, or satisfaction, or necessary sacrifice. They did not know the feeling of taking a place and keeping it, securing a village and then raising the flag and calling it a victory. No sense of order or momentum. No front, no rear, no trenches laid out in neat parallels. No Patton rushing for the Rhine, no beachheads to storm and win and hold for the duration. They did not have tar-

gets. They did not have a cause. They did not know if it was a war of ideology or economics or hegemony or spite.... They did not know the names of most villages. They did not know which villages were critical. They did not know strategies. They did not know the terms of the war, the rules of fair play. When they took prisoners, which was rare, they did not know the questions to ask, whether to release a suspect or beat on him. They did not know how to feel. Whether, when seeing a dead Vietnamese, to be happy or sad or relieved; whether, in times of quiet, to be apprehensive or content; whether to engage the enemy or elude him. They did not know how to feel when they saw villages burning. Revenge? Loss? Peace of mind or anguish? They did not know.... Magic, mystery, ghosts and incense, whispers in the dark, strange tongues and strange smells, uncertainties never articulated in war stories, emotion squandered on ignorance. They did not know good from evil.[11]

This passage emphasizes the discontinuity between this war and America's previous wars. Little wonder that the phrase "It don't mean nothin' " became a litany in Vietnam, for the experience was so overwhelming that the soldier lacked the language and the concepts to explain it. "It don't mean nothin' " signifies circuit overload, both a negation of all previous meaning and an excess of new meaning, a psychic numbing so profound that neither the words nor the will can be found to make sense of it. The phrase applies not only to personal life — a loss of individual purpose — but also to social life, the loss of the *meaning* of America, America as an idea, as an ideal, as a coherent system of hopes, aspirations, and possibilities.

Few presidents have been as gifted as John F. Kennedy in capturing the essence of America's dominant story. His New Frontier rejuvenated a nation stymied by cold war frustration. It provided something for everyone. The space program excited the scientists, the Peace Corps tapped a vast reservoir of goodwill toward new nations, and the Green Berets mobilized youthful dreams of reliving the adventures of the Old West. Because of the powerful emotional elements embodied in the national story, the rejuvenation of frontier myths engendered deep commitment and sometimes immense sacrifice. But in Vietnam the American story backfired. Science and technology proved insufficient; nation-building was ineffectual; and American "cowboys" met "Indians" they could not defeat. Because expectations had been raised so high, defeat took on a symbolic meaning of its own, far beyond the scope of Vietnam. "On the deepest level, the legacy of Vietnam is the disruption of our story, of our explanation of the past and vision of the future."[12]

Loren Baritz uses the term "American Exceptionalism" to describe the controlling myths of U.S. national identity and purpose.[13] These are clearly utopian and have their origin in certain stories of the New England Pilgrims, although each generation of American leaders is free to graft on new elements as historical circumstances require. The myths include a variety of diverse elements: innocence, purity, uniqueness, superiority, invincibility, a conflict between good and evil (civilization versus wilderness, cowboy versus Indian, and so on), limitless possibilities, a "can-do" optimism, and regeneration through violence. America would be different — an exception — from the corrupt and oppressive societies of the Old World. The devout Pilgrims entered into a covenant with God to be the New Israel, God's chosen people, embarking on a fresh start in history in a new world. This New Adam would embark on an "errand into the wilderness" to open up a virgin continent and bring the blessings of Christian civilization to its savage natives.[14]

The frontier western and the Indian wars form the narrative pattern of myths that would be adapted to new situations as the experiences of the European settlers changed over time. America would be a city set on a hill, a light to the nations — a concept that in time would be transformed into Manifest Destiny, a form of messianic nationalism that justifies imperial expansion.[15] In the nineteenth and twentieth centuries the idea of technological progress would be added to the myths, and even though the myths would be secularized, America's divine mission gained a fresh teleological thrust in history.[16]

Innocence, uniqueness, purity, benevolence, superiority, invincibility, defense of the oppressed — whatever the combination of virtues, orators down through U.S. history have pointed to the moral high ground of American identity. In *White Jacket*, novelist Herman Melville gave expression to one aspect of the myth: "And we Americans are the peculiar, chosen people — the Israel of our time; we bear the ark of the liberties of the world."[17] President Wilson repeated it more blatantly when he declared at Versailles after World War I, "At last the world knows America as the savior of the world!"[18] When the last American troops were leaving Vietnam, the New Testament scholar Robert Jewett published a study showing the biblical roots of American political messianism. He entitled it, appropriately, *The Captain America Complex*.[19]

Two components of the myth have been linked historically in a particularly nefarious manner: the division of the world into two camps — one good, the other evil — and the necessity of violence to produce the good. This Manichaean division of the world into good guys/bad guys forms the fundamental worldview of the frontier western, robing violence in a righteous mantle. The reluctant hero is forced to use violence, but he does so in a minimalist manner, using only that amount of violence that is necessary to restore justice. While the villain uses all kinds of dirty tactics, the hero retains his integrity in the midst of violence because of his constraint. This selective violence then brings renewal to the frontier settlement that had been threatened by the uncontrolled violence of the wilderness. Thus, the willingness to use violence becomes a mark of courage and virtue for the hero, whose personal motives are above reproach.

In this manner American use of force becomes an exercise in virtue and our wars take on the righteousness of crusades. President Wilson earned the reputation of an idealistic crusader with such statements as, "When men take up arms to set other men free, there is something sacred and holy in the warfare. I will not cry 'peace' as long as there is sin and wrong in the world." Thirty-five years later a hard-nosed general-turned-president, Eisenhower, would echo this perspective in his 1953 inaugural address: "The forces of good and evil are massed and armed and opposed as rarely before in history." When his turn at the helm of state came, President Kennedy would describe the defense of freedom and human rights around the world as "God's work."[20] And in 1991 President Bush would use the same Manichaean categories to mobilize American support for Desert Storm.

I find it helpful to diagram this complex web of national myths to show their mutual support and interconnections (see fig. 6, below). When the web of myths that has formed the traditional American identity is displayed in this fashion, it appears somewhat ludicrous, a collective version of the ancient prayer, "Oh God, I thank thee that I am not like other men." We expect myths to be simplifications of reality because we know that by their very nature myths embody selective dimensions of experience and aspiration. But when these myths are examined rationally, they have an almost comic book quality, like Captain America. Nevertheless, this web of myths, this historical embodiment of corporate self-righteousness, has been reinforced by almost four hundred years of Indian wars, the conquest of a virgin continent, the development of unparalleled economic productivity, and national experience in two world wars. It is so deeply ingrained in American popular culture and functions at such an unconscious emotive level that only the most devastating of experiences can shake our confidence in it. Indeed, this is the web of myths that American GIs took with them to Vietnam and by which

Figure 6
American Exceptionalism

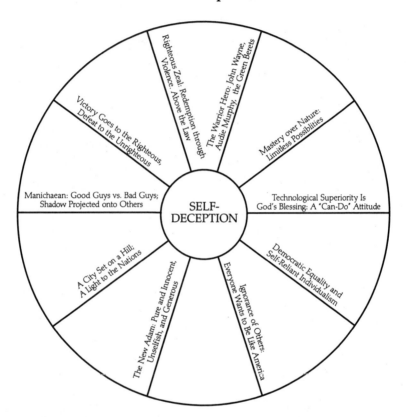

they interpreted their experiences there. It was the Wild
West all over again.

G. K. Chesterton once remarked that America is a "nation with the soul of a church." Sydney Mead has explored
the process whereby the United States as a nation acquired
the sacred qualities of a religious body.[21] The original New
England Puritans had no intention of separating religion
from politics. Their settlement was to be a holy common-

wealth where the laws of society would embody the laws of God. Politics and religion were extensions of each other.

Later on, when the existence of diverse denominations required the disestablishment of one church and the formal recognition of religious pluralism, the state became the arbiter in disputes between denominations, thereby gaining prestige at the expense of religious bodies. The denomination could no longer make exclusive claims to be the New Israel of God's elect. Instead, denominations were turned into voluntary societies. The aura of sacred authority was then transferred to the nation itself, which began to function like a church in three ways. First, denominations were pushed more and more into the private sphere, while the nation took over the primary role as the agent of God's meaningful activity in history. Second, the nation took over from the denominations as the primary source of personal and group identity. We became Americans first and members of this or that religious organization second. Finally, the nation also assumed a religious function by becoming itself a community of righteousness. This process is usually described by historians in positive terms as the institutionalization of religious freedom and the end of the wars of religion. What is often forgotten is the negative side. National myths present an idealized past sanitized from error, sin, and failure. National ceremonies celebrate our glorious corporate ventures. As we learned in the Vietnam War, no president is willing to admit defeat or error. Thus, in the absence of rituals of confession or a common religious perspective that would call the nation to repentance, the national story rarely comes under judgment. Instead, the religious characteristics of our corporate identity mask raw national power. Particular national interest parades as universal good. Most Americans do not see this as national idolatry because religion has been so privatized, leaving the nation free from religious critique and accountability. When young GIs were called to risk their lives in war, they naturally assumed that they were fighting for a righteous cause. When the cause failed, the worldview that sustained it also crumbled.

Perhaps the most provocative metaphor for the demise of the American myth is the journey taken by a central character in Tim O'Brien's novel *Going after Cacciato*. While on guard duty on the perimeter of his unit one night, foot soldier Paul Berlin decides to explore in his imagination what other alternatives might be available. Another soldier, Cacciato, has gone AWOL into Laos. Berlin, who is thoroughly disillusioned with the war, begins to imagine what it would be like for a squad of men to go in pursuit of Cacciato. Would they be doing their duty, trying to capture a deserter? Or would the pursuit be an excuse for their desertion as well? Thus, Berlin and several others embark on an imaginary journey in pursuit of Cacciato, who leads and eludes them all the way west, to Paris. This is a westward journey that inverts the American story. The hero has deserted the myth, and the journey leads back to the corrupt and oppressive Old World, where peace talks have broken down. Pushed to its logical conclusion, the American myth has come full circle. The hero renounces regeneration through violence, but peace is not yet at hand. At the end of the novel, Cacciato is missing in action. The future of the American myth and its hero remains uncertain.[22]

We are now in a position to assess the full dimensions of the phrase, "It don't mean nothin'." Over forty years ago Arthur Koestler wrote of the profound disillusionment experienced by young communists when their utopian dream was transformed into a Stalinist gulag. He entitled the story *The God That Failed*.[23] A god that fails is an idol, a set of beliefs and values that is helpful and good in its place — like patriotism — but that becomes harmful and evil when allowed to claim uncritical, ultimate loyalty. In the Vietnam War we face nothing less than the death of an idol and the devastating price paid for idolatry. In Vietnam "Americanism" failed.[24] Power, innocence, purity, organization, technology, can-do optimism, heroism, the defense of civilization — the whole myth turned in upon itself. How ironic! Self-destruction by "friendly fire." The resulting crisis, the so-called Vietnam syndrome, is really the loss of national identity because the national story — the national *theology* — is no longer credible. The web of myths that holds that story together has come unraveled.

When a god fails, scapegoating is one defense. Many veterans and others find convenient scapegoats in the press or the antiwar movement or in the Pentagon and the White House, which put restrictions on military strategy. But scapegoating is self-deceptive. It leaves a residual uneasiness because of the knowledge, even if at a barely conscious level, of dissimulation. In fact, one of the reasons that "Americanism" has a hollow ring is that the paradigmatic American myth is itself a scapegoat formula. The "savage" qualities of the American soul are projected onto national enemies and then exorcised by killing them.

Another defensive response to the death of a national god grows naturally from the American can-do spirit. Rather than recognize the limits of power and the inability to achieve political goals through force alone, we redouble our efforts. The *Rambo* films present this strategy. But torquing up the level of violence merely destroys the human qualities of the hero himself. Desert Storm provides an example in real life. No stone was left unturned. The most advanced weaponry was massively deployed to obliterate enemy forces, many of them in a "turkey shoot." In order to ensure a decisive victory, one hundred thousand Iraqi civilians were killed, four million Kurds became refugees, and the infrastructure of an entire country was laid waste. The bravado surrounding celebrations and parades for American troops returning home rang hollow, for American pride is inherently unstable if it must be purchased at the cost of callous disregard for innocent Iraqis and Kurds.

Scapegoating and redoubling the effort, both attempts at avoidance and denial, are cowardly refusals to face the truth because facing the truth requires the admission that the national god has failed. Admission of the failure of the national god leads to recognition of a crisis in national identity and also a crisis in personal identity insofar as it is based upon national identity. "It don't mean nothin'" is the result. In reality, "it" means everything, for meaning itself, the will to meaning, has been frustrated. Over eight hundred thousand of the three million troops who served in Vietnam suffer from what the Veterans Administration calls a psychiatric illness, post–traumatic stress disorder. The symptoms include nightmares, depression, isolation, rage, guilt, psychic numbing, and various forms of dysfunctional behavior. In reality, the vets suffer the psychiatric symptoms of a profound spiritual illness.

The Demise of Faith, Hope, and Love

Peter Marin has challenged the adequacy of the term "traumatic stress" to describe what he believes is "moral pain."[25] He maintains that a purely psychological approach to war's ravages of the soul is inadequate because of the therapist's neglect of the moral dimension of personhood. My impression is that a major dimension of moral pain is the frustration of the will to meaning. This takes the form of a loss of faith, hope, and love, which are essential for purposeful life.

In Christian tradition these have been called the theological or the supernatural virtues, which grace adds to the natural virtues of prudence, justice, courage, and temperance. Years ago Emil Brunner published a series of lectures in which he pointed out that faith, hope, and love are not "virtues" but dimensions of right-relatedness to the past, the future, and the present. "We live in the past by faith; we live in the future by hope; we live in the present by love."[26] Whereas Brunner analyzes faith, hope, and love in Christian terms, I believe it is possible to regard these as universal human dimensions of meaningful life everywhere.

We live simultaneously in the past, the future, and the

present. The past is with us now as memory, the future as anticipation. The three dimensions coexist as "tensed modalities" of consciousness.[27] Let us examine each of these dimensions. When we say we live in the past by faith, we mean that the past is the ground on which we stand, our source of trust, the basis of our faith in the order and goodness of life, the bedrock of our belief that life is meaningful. Another way of putting it is to say that faith is the knowledge of being loved in the past, of being in right relationship with others and with the world, and therefore is the experience of joy in the past.

We all understand this at the personal level. But personal faith also has a corporate dimension. Faith is the knowledge that the national narrative that shapes personal identity is reliable, worthy of trust. The more our identity is shaped by Americanism rather than a transnational commitment to the universal community of humankind, the more important will be the national narrative. If that national narrative has no place for sin, guilt, and forgiveness, for failure, grief, and healing (dimensions of the past that live in the present by memory), the faith it instills will be shallow.

We live in the future by anticipation. Anticipation may be hopeful or fearful and anxious, depending in part upon the quality of our faith. When the Enlightenment banished God and enthroned humans as agents of our own destiny, a progressive teleology replaced Christian hope. Planning (science and technology) became the source of hope. When planning fails, as it did in Vietnam, the illusion of human control over the future is shattered, and security is replaced by fear and anxiety. Hope is the expectation of good things in the future, a "leaning into" the future with eager openness. When young men and women of nineteen or twenty experience the destruction of their faith, their hope in the future likewise shrivels.

Love is full openness to the present. Because our present is haunted by the memory of our past — whether it be from guilt or anger or low self-esteem or whatever — and clouded by our anxiety and fear of the future, we are not fully open. Instead, we turn in upon ourselves. Depression is only the extreme form of what is the normal human condition, the closing off of full openness to the present. In veterans this takes the form of psychic numbing, the inability to develop fulfilling intimate relationships, the absence of spontaneous joy.

Another way of describing the loss of faith, hope, and love is merely the declaration that God is dead, or as some vets say, "God went AWOL in Vietnam." Ron Kovic puts it in these terms: "After the war...there was very little left of a country for me. There was very little left of a mother and a father and sisters and brothers, family; the war shattered all of that. There was just me, alive and breathing every single day, trying to make sense of this madness. What does it mean to really be dead, to lose everything, because I don't believe in God? There is no God for me after Vietnam."[28] This is a clear confession, echoed by many vets, that Americanism is an idol, a god that failed.

The Price of Denial

The magnitude of the threat to Americanism posed by the military defeat in Vietnam can be measured by the intensity of denial that followed the war. After the fall of Saigon and the evacuation of all Americans from South Vietnam in 1975, the nation at large wanted to put to rest the war and all its divisiveness. No wonder the vets went underground, for their very presence evoked hostility and shameful memories. Certain scholars embarked upon revisionist histories of the war; the film industry followed suit with the *Rambo* series; and Presidents Reagan and Bush sought opportunities for military intervention abroad in order to prove that nothing had been changed by the outcome of the American war in Vietnam.

Denial did not begin only after the war. The war itself was a form of denial of Asian and American realities. The official lies that persisted from beginning to end denote an overall pattern of duplicity and self-deception.[29] Between 1969 and 1975, David Rabe, a brilliant young playwright who served in Vietnam during the mid-1960s, produced three plays focusing on different aspects of the war. The most celebrated of the three, *Sticks and Bones,* won the Tony Award in 1972 for the best play on Broadway.[30] Beneath a straightforward story of the difficulties a veteran faces in reintegrating into his family upon his return from the war lurks one of the most devastating allegories of our time, depicting the collision of narratives and the lethal behavior that flows from certain myths embedded in the American narrative. Few other works calculate so clearly the cost of the projection of national evil upon one's enemies and the ensuing denial and self-deception. And rarely has the irony been presented more graphically: only the blind can see, only the wounded can heal.

Sticks and Bones is set in the bright, modern home of Ozzie and Harriet Nelson and their son Ricky, characters whom Rabe takes from a 1950s television sitcom depicting a happy and superficial American family of consumers. Rabe examines two intertwining themes — sickness and blindness — to demonstrate the extreme to which a family (and by extension a nation) will go to preserve its optimistic but destructive self-image. In the author's note that precedes the script, Rabe writes: "In any society there is an image of how the perfectly happy family should appear. It is this image that the people in this play wish to preserve above all else. Mom and Dad are not concerned that terrible events have occurred in the world, but rather that David has come home to behave in a manner that makes him no longer lovable. Thus he is keeping them from being the happy family they know they must be. He attacks those aspects of their self-image in which reside all their sense of value and sanity."

The play opens with the return of David, the older son, from service in Vietnam. He has been blinded in the war. A sergeant major dumps him back home like a piece of merchandise, demanding a signature on the shipping receipt. At first David does not recognize his family, a sign of the alienation that exists between vets and the rest of the nation. Each character reinforces the alienation just by playing the role of a typical American family member. Harriet, the ever-solicitous mother/wife, is always ready to cover over any domestic ripple with cheerful advice, a sleeping pill, a magical blessing from Father Donald, or another piece of fudge. Even when she focuses on David's unhappiness, the deepest level of analysis she is capable of is the conclusion that David suffers from guilt because he broke the sixth commandment by sleeping with a whore. Ricky, David's seventeen-year-old brother, is sealed in an adolescent cocoon of guitar music, cars, sports, and perpetual activity. At the least little sign of conflict or even serious conversation, he escapes to the kitchen, to bed, or to the next engagement outside the home.

Ozzie is more complex. He too is trapped in the cultural superficiality of cheerful consumerism — at one point he asserts his self-worth by tallying up all his possessions. Although he finds escape in television and nostalgic reveries of his youthful athletic prowess, Ozzie is jealous of his son's wartime adventure. He suspects that David may have achieved a success that has eluded him and may possess a knowledge hidden from him. This vulnerability makes Ozzie all the more defensive as father and son lock in on a clash of narratives, symbolic of the generational antagonism in the country at large.

David wants little more than a hearing, so that he can explore his wartime experiences, the myths that led him into war and turned him into a killer, the racism that allowed him to maim and kill Vietnamese with pleasure. But the other family members want to suppress his memories and deny any connection between the war and their way of life. Though blind, David sees things that the family cannot or will not see. He shows a film of two mutilated bodies, hanging from trees, but they reply, "David, there's nothing there." He describes the scene in detail:

"They hang by their wrists half-severed by the wire,... he with the back of his head blown off and she, the rifle jammed exactly and deeply into her, with a bullet fired directly into the child living there." Harriet replies automatically: "It's so awful the things those yellow people do to one another.... David, don't let it hurt you. All the things you saw... It's inhuman, barbaric and uncivilized and inhuman" (p. 260).

David makes a second attempt at confession: "Because I talk of certain things... don't think I did them. Murderers don't even know that murder happens." At this Ricky runs upstairs to bed while Harriet, fearful that she might understand, begs David: "What are you saying? No, no. We're a family, that's all — we've had a little trouble — David, you've got to stop.... Just be happy and home like all the others" (pp. 260–61).

When confession fails David delves deeper into the origin of his views and values and realizes that the collision of narratives is so profound that it's either kill or be killed; either their view of life, or his own. With new-found confidence David addresses his brother: "To see you die is why I live, Rick," thus giving voice to the vet's sense of mission to alter the national narrative. To Ozzie, David whispers, "I think you should know I've begun to hate you. I feel the wound of you, yet I don't think you can tell me any more. I... must tell you" (p. 264). The roles reverse as David assumes his new responsibility. "In time I'll show you some things. You'll see them. I will be your father" (p. 273).

The play pivots on the role of Zung, the Vietnamese lover whom David has left behind, but who, as an apparition only he can see, drifts in and out from scene to scene. When David tells his family about her, they call her a "yellow whore." When they learn that he truly loves Zung, Harriet vomits and Ozzie attacks David, slapping him repeatedly: *"LITTLE BITTY CHINKY KIDS HE WANTED TO HAVE! LITTLE BITTY CHINKY KIDS! DIDN'T YOU! FOR OUR GRANDCHILDREN!"* (p. 265).

For David this racist heritage lies at the root of the war,

for the obliteration of one people by another cannot occur unless the enemy is first rendered less than human. Thus the apparition of Zung is a projection of David's guilt both for the killing he did and also for abandoning her. "I discarded you," he tells her. "Forgive me. . . . Zung, there were old voices inside me I had trusted all my life as if they were my own. I didn't know I shouldn't hear them. So reasonable and calm they seemed a source of wisdom. 'She's all of everything impossible made possible, cast her down,' they said. 'Go home.' And I did as they told" (p. 266).

But Zung is also the source of David's transformation, for in their love is revealed the destructive quality of his cultural heritage and military training. "They were all just hunks of meat that had no mind to know of me until I cared for her" (p. 272), says David, echoing other vets who report that when they began seeing the enemy as human, they lost their effectiveness as killers. Thus, Zung also represents the source of redemption from David's past. In the encounter with Zung, David (like America) is presented with the opportunity to embrace his shadow and become whole again. Two voices compete for dominance within his soul, the voice of personal experience ("She's the thing most possibly of value in my life") and the voice of his cultural heritage ("She is garbage and filth"). Yet David knows, "I must get her back if I wish to live. Sickness, I must cherish her" (p. 266). Later in the play, when Ozzie's worldview is coming unglued under David's relentless attack, David repeats this statement but enlarges its meaning by directing it to Ozzie and, by extension, to America at large. "She is garbage and filth, and *you* must get her back if *you* wish to live" (p. 280; emphasis added).

The lines are clearly drawn. The two conflicting narratives cannot coexist. For both David and his family, it's either kill or be killed. The author's own despair finds expression in the last scene. Ricky complains, "Mom, [David is] driving Dad crazy" (p. 280). In a final struggle to resist the transformation of his own worldview, Ozzie seizes Zung by the throat — this is the first time he has been able to see her — and strangles her, thus extinguishing any revelation she might bring and any chance for growth on his part. Then all three declare that David is crazy and should die. Earlier David had predicted as much, telling his father, "It's only fraud that keeps us sane" (p. 264). "They will call it madness. We will call it seeing" (p. 280). Together they assist David in slitting his wrists, a reference to the innumerable socially induced suicides among Vietnam vets. Rather than alter their own facile and destructive view of things, they sacrifice their own son/brother, whose new story would nullify their old one. In this manner an entire generation of youth is sacrificed to ward off any threat to the national self-image.

Rabe indeed demonstrated his clairvoyance in portraying David's fate, for the play itself received similar treatment. CBS scheduled it for nationwide showing in 1973 but then canceled it for fear of offending public sensitivities when American POWs were being released in Hanoi. Later, after much protest by Rabe and other vets, it was actually broadcast, but over half of the CBS-affiliated stations refused to show it.

The price of denial is death. To recover from the death of a dream, the poet must first take us "right to the bottom of the night." Rabe takes us on that journey, recognizing that unless we embrace the darkness into which we have stumbled, we can find no way out.

Chapter Six

The Dark Night

[T]he most insidious and intimate battle...[is] the one with yourself.

—Charles Coleman, *Sergeant Back Again*

Healing the Wound Lightly

Marilyn told us at the beginning of the semester that she signed up for the course to learn about the war that had so warped her father's life. During the first few class sessions she remained quiet but attentive to others' stories. Then one evening before class she approached me somewhat timidly, yet full of emotion. "I, uh,...I want to read my journal tonight...to the whole class. OK?"

So we started the class with Marilyn's story. Her father had been in therapy on and off for much of her life, but he never seemed to change. Whenever she asked him about the war, his eyes would glaze over and fixate on some distant object. "For my father, the war never ended but only moved to his mind, haunting him with bad memories forever," she had concluded. Then one evening her group of friends decided to see the film *Platoon*. She begged them to choose a different movie, but they insisted and she went along. "Soon the screen became a complete jungle that sucked me in. Now all of the feelings and experiences that I felt my father had been hiding from me were being shown. I could hardly bear to look at the screen because I didn't want to see what I was seeing. It was horrifying. I blocked out everything with one exception: Every soldier's face be-

128

longed to my father, including the mutilated corpses. The scenes made me sick. One second he was being blown to pieces, the next he was the killer. I could not stand it any longer and abruptly left the theater."

When she approached her father again, he replied: "I have told you all you need to know. The rest shall be buried with me.... No one will ever understand. No movie or book can possibly make people understand what hell we went through.... It's too late for society to make up for it now.... One minute you're holding your buddy's dead body, the next minute you're throwing a load of groceries on the shelf. Please, let it lay, don't ask me anymore.... I need you to let it go, I need to let it go." After some moments of silence, as if to end the conversation, Marilyn's father said wistfully, "There's nothing like the undying spirit of the grunt. One fine day we shall meet on our grey horses and get the job done right."

"That's all he would tell me," said Marilyn. "He can't put it behind him, and neither can I."

Marilyn's story illustrates how her father's wounds have been "healed lightly."[1] While viewing the movie *Platoon* she saw him as both killer and killed, an indication that she had picked up his own unconscious ambivalence about his role in the war. Verbally, all he had ever communicated was his feeling of entrapment and betrayal: "It's too late for society to make up for it now." But in other more indirect ways he must have communicated his guilt; otherwise she would not have seen his face in the film as killer. This substantiates the comment of Walter Capps: "Every Vietnam veteran I have met who killed someone in the war carries a burden of guilt."[2] It also confirms the observation of psychiatrist Robert Lifton, who has noted that in their dreams many vets see themselves simultaneously as victim and executioner.[3]

On the other hand, the father's final declaration conveys personal responsibility for failure: "One fine day we shall ... get the job done right." Since failure is related more to shame than to guilt, both of which convey a sense of personal responsibility, therapists who assume that the resolution of guilt is the primary key to healing would benefit from more recent studies of shame.[4] The more prominent conscious problem for Marilyn's father is loss of self-esteem as a result of his inability to live up to the ideal of the "spirit of the grunt."

Unfortunately, this self-analysis of the problem will never lead to healing because the ideal itself is defective and merely exacerbates the suffering. Lacking an alternative ideal or narrative, this man is trapped in a never-ending spiral of self-condemnation.

At some level combat vets sense this dual experience of being simultaneously victims and executioners. The standard help provided to vets does not deal adequately with either of these experiences. In fact, by naming their "illness" post–traumatic stress disorder (PTSD), the diagnostic process participates in the evil from which they suffer, for the diagnosis is itself a form of denial, a cover-up of the real sources of their wounds. Some veterans' organizations spend much energy decrying the lack of adequate benefits for vets, but by accepting the diagnostic categories provided by the therapeutic community and the VA hospitals, they too join the cover-up and perpetuate the betrayal. This is a strong charge to level against these institutions. To substantiate the claim that the PTSD diagnosis treats the symptoms while neglecting the underlying causes for the vets' dual experience of responsibility/guilt and betrayal/anger, we need to examine PTSD more closely.

Post–Traumatic Stress Disorder

Toward the end of World War I military psychiatrists realized that what had been known as shell shock was due not to physiological damage to the brain but rather to the emotional trauma of battle and war-related events. Diagnosis shifted to "combat neurosis," then "combat exhaustion" or "battle fatigue." The 365-day tour of duty and midterm

R & R in Vietnam were designed to reduce the incidence of combat exhaustion. This policy succeeded merely in delaying the onset of severe disorders until soldiers had returned home or retired from the military.

By the end of the 1970s the number of veterans suffering from a variety of symptoms — depression, rage, bouts of violence, suicidal thoughts, flashbacks, nightmares, sleep disorders, startle reactions, fear, isolation and alienation, incapacity for intimate relationships, problems with authority, psychic numbing, self-denigration, survivor guilt and related difficulties — was so massive that a new psychiatric category, PTSD, was added to the standard diagnostic manual published by the American Psychiatric Association, the *DSM, III*. A 1988 study by the Research Triangle in North Carolina estimated that 31 percent (830,000) of all Vietnam vets have suffered from PTSD.[5]

M. J. Horowitz developed the diagnostic model — called the bi-phasic trauma response syndrome — most widely used in treatment programs.[6] A traumatic event triggers anxiety. In order to cope the person develops defenses to reduce the anxiety. These include various forms of detachment like psychic numbing, loss of memory, and other forms of repression or denial. When these defenses begin to break down, as they inevitably do over a period of time, the victim may seek to prolong the avoidance by turning to alcohol and drugs or other forms of flight. The literature is filled with stories of the elaborate lengths to which vets will go to avoid reminders of painful war experiences.

Treatment of all but the most severe cases usually involves introducing the vet into a "rap group" of other vets where four tasks must be undertaken: to *remember* the past, to reexperience the trauma and anxiety of the past by *recounting* it in the presence of others, to *confront* the unresolved issues that arise from the past, and finally to *reinterpret* the past.[7] Herein lies the problem. Because the therapeutic model of reality is so limited, major dimensions of the suffering are left unexplored and misinterpreted. An interview I had with Ruth, a senior army officer and Vietnam veteran nurse, illustrates the point. She had been working in vet rehabilitation ever since the war. Here is the conversation about the adequacy of the term "PTSD."

Q: I've sifted through the literature and talked with many vets. It seems that many different reasons are given for PTSD:

1. the trauma of battle or battle-related events;

2. guilt for killing and guilt for surviving while buddies were killed;

3. the evil nature of the war itself ("The war was fucked," as the grunts put it);

4. anger at official American hypocrisy and loss of faith in the idea of America;

5. abandonment by God ("God went AWOL in Vietnam"); and

6. a sense of betrayal by the nation as a whole ("One group blamed us for fighting, another group blamed us for not winning, when in fact they prevented us from doing what was necessary to win. We are nothing more than scapegoats").

In your experience, which of these elements contribute to the symptoms described as PTSD?

A: Not every veteran I see suffers from all of these, but most suffer from a combination of causes.

Q: Which of these causes do you treat?

A: Well, officially we treat trauma ... or at least the symptoms which result from trauma.

Q: What do you mean "officially"? Do you deal with other things "unofficially"?

A: We can't get into the other causes you mention because we are government institutions of the Veterans Administration. Officially we don't get involved in the morality of the war or religious questions. We leave that to the chaplains.

Q: But unofficially you do?

A: Sure we do. They're all related. You can't separate them. In the rap groups vets discuss whatever they feel like discussing. Actually, among the therapists there are two different opinions. The dominant one — and the one that operates in the VA system — is that you deal with the symptoms of PTSD first, and then later the vets can deal with issues of morality and religion on their own. That's supposed to be more "scientific." The other view is that there's no way to separate the symptoms from the causes. That's the approach I take.

Q: Even though it's not the official VA position? Aren't you being a bit subversive?

A: Look, the VA is abusive. It scapegoats the vets. I try to make an inhuman system a bit more human. That's the least I can do for those who served their country and then were abandoned by their country. Sure, it's subversive. It has to be.

Because treatment is dependent upon diagnosis, we should note five interrelated dimensions of defective diagnosis. First, PTSD is a *misnomer*. Much of the suffering of vets is not traumatic or delayed but chronic and nontraumatic. The vets I interviewed have recovered from most of the symptoms associated with PTSD, but they still suffer from an indefinable emptiness. Walter Capps reported his conversation with veteran Larry Heinemann, the award-winning novelist. "I have a hole in my heart," said Heinemann. "A place that's dead. I'll never get it back. Just ask my wife."[8] Loss of faith, hope, and love, the loss of *élan vital* that we discussed in chapter 4, is left untouched when the problem is named in such narrow terms and treatment is confined to the narrow discipline of psychiatry.

Second, another way of putting this is that existing psy-

chiatric therapy is *reductionistic*. It substitutes a part for the
whole. Focusing on physiological and psychological symptoms apart from their moral and religious causes is like
attacking water pollution with a filter system downstream
while factories continue to discharge pollutants upstream.
As we noted earlier, Peter Marin insists that vets suffer a
form of "moral pain" that is ignored when the label PTSD
is assigned to their problems.[9] Because the nation as a
whole has been unwilling or unable to deal with the moral
and spiritual dimensions of the war, a government agency
like the Veterans Administration is not in a position to deal
with them either. When its employees like Ruth do so, they
feel uneasy and angry, as if they were acting subversively.

Third, the result of substituting a part for the whole is
that the vets' suffering is *privatized*. Traditionally psychotherapy has focused on the self as the unit of analysis
and treatment, neglecting to some degree the larger social and cultural systems to which the self belongs and
that contribute to the very constitution of the self. In the
interview above, Ruth declared that the Veterans Administration abuses Vietnam vets by making them scapegoats.
When I probed this issue, she explained: "It's the government and the country at large that suffer from PTSD: anger,
guilt, shame, denial, mistrust, and all the rest. We've been
saying that for years. It's good politics to blame the victims. Then America avoids the consequences of its own
actions and condemns the veterans to pay the price."[10]

Fourth, by privatizing the suffering, PTSD also *depoliti-
cizes* war-related problems. Thus, the nation avoids facing the demonic dimensions of American Exceptionalism
that fuel our wars; society is absolved of any responsibility for perpetuating a culture of violence where "real
men" become killers; politicians and the military escape
accountability for lies and cover-ups; and subsequent ad-
ministrations are able to manipulate foreign affairs so as
to "put the Vietnam syndrome behind us once and for
all." In so doing, the official "lessons" learned from that
war are limited to strategic and tactical military matters,

divorced from the larger framework of human meaning. The officially commissioned study of the American war in Vietnam by Colonel Harry G. Summers, Jr., entitled *On Strategy*, illustrates such a limited perspective.[11] In this manner the next generation of youth are trained once more to sacrifice themselves unquestioningly to a devouring nationalistic god.

Finally, the diagnostic category PTSD ignores the fact that *emotions are narrative-dependent*. In this sense, not much diagnostic progress has been made since World War I. In that war shell shock was defined as damage to the brain, a purely mechanical phenomenon that affected individuals differently, depending upon their physiological strength and resilience. Similarly, PTSD is also regarded in mechanical terms, except that now the "illness" caused by trauma is said to be emotional rather than physiological. As a result, the age-old tendency to regard the victims as "malingerers" or "whiners" or "wimps" who are weak in character is reenforced. In an interview with a former vet chaplain, I asked why a third of the nation's homeless are Vietnam veterans, many of whom suffer from PTSD. "It has very little to do with the war," he replied. "Those guys were losers from the beginning. They just couldn't hack it in Vietnam. Even if they hadn't been in the war, they'd still be street people." Then he told me with considerable pride about his own wound, the loss of a limb, and how he had recovered with no remorse. "I never even looked back." When I learned that he had been a top official in the Veterans Administration, I began to understand some of the rage that other vets feel toward the VA system.

What does it mean to say that emotions are narrative-dependent? Martha Nussbaum explains: "[E]motions are not feelings that well up in some natural and untutored way from our natural selves. . . . [T]hey are, in fact, not personal or natural at all. . . . [T]hey are, instead, contrivances, social constructs. We learn how to feel, and we learn our emotional repertoire. We learn our emotions in the same way that we learn our beliefs — from our society. . . . They are taught, above all, through stories. Stories express their structure and teach us their dynamics.... [O]nce internalized ... [these stories] shape the way life feels and looks."[12]

A dramatic personal experience in 1992 brought home to me the narrative unity of cognition and emotion. I had taken a seminary class to Vietnam and Cambodia to examine our postwar responsibilities at a time when U.S. relations with the region were improving. In Cambodia we saw reminders of the Khmer Rouge madness in which over two million people were slaughtered in the latter half of the 1970s — the near-total destruction of an entire national culture. Our pilgrimage to the prison at Toul Sleng High School and the death camp at Choeung Ek reminded me of similar visits to Nazi concentration camps in Europe and conversations with relatives of Jewish survivors of the Holocaust. Then we visited the supreme patriarch of Theravada Buddhism in Cambodia. Of the top forty-seven leaders in the hierarchy before the Khmer Rouge seized power, he alone escaped execution. After his survey of the war and the current state of Buddhism in his country, we asked for his theological interpretation of the Cambodian "killing fields." His response was one of sadness, tempered by peaceful resignation. It had none of the moral outrage that accompanies tales of the Holocaust. I can only attribute this to the difference in religious narratives whereby Judaism inculcates prophetic protest against evil while Buddhism engenders acquiescence.

If vets are to accomplish the fourth and final task of healing, namely that of *reinterpretation*, then they must move beyond any therapy that substitutes a part for the whole and severs the relationship between emotion and belief, between feeling and meaning, which together are embedded in narrative — for any such therapy actually *prevents* recovery. In fact, such a therapy is a form of denial, a lie that perpetuates the betrayal and victimization of vets. The diagnosis itself keeps them both guilty and angry, responsible and betrayed. It may alleviate some of the symptoms, but it cannot deliver the patient from captivity to emotionally damaging ways of understanding the world. No wonder Marilyn's father has been in and out of therapy for many years, without any significant change. He remains stuck in the same story of the "spirit of the grunt," in spite of the fact that this story failed in Vietnam and still feeds his inner sense of shame.

Reinterpretation requires replacing an inadequate story with one that restructures the traumatic events into a different pattern of meaning. Because "emotion itself is the acceptance of, the assent to live according to, a certain sort of story,"[13] no recovery is adequate until the old narrative is replaced by a new one. And since personal narratives are dependent upon societal narratives, reinterpretation of the one requires reconstruction of the other. Vets have experienced a different story, but society does not confirm or reinforce it. And many are not able to disentangle the features of their new experience from the expectations of the old story. By furnishing a privatized and depoliticized definition of their turmoil, the Veterans Administration and the mental health professions imprison vets in the old narrative, a socially defined "disorder" of failures that prevents healing. At the same time, the nation is protected from the necessity of confessing its own failure and betrayal, as well as from the arduous task of reconstructing a new narrative.

"If stories are learned, they can be unlearned. If emotions are constructs, they can be dismantled.... [If emotions] rest upon beliefs, then they can be modified by a modification of belief."[14] Each of the first four features cited above in our critique of PTSD — misnaming, reducing the whole to a part, privatizing, and depoliticizing — derives from the failure to recognize the narrative-based quality of emotions and the necessity for a narrative-based therapy. Once emotional disorders are examined in terms of the narratives that give rise to them, treatment requires a holistic enterprise that unites physiology, psychology, morality, and religion in such a way that the sufferings of the self are related to the larger narrative of society. Arthur

Egendorf, a former CIA officer in Vietnam and now a therapist working with vets, offers a similar critique of the PTSD "industry" when he declares that healing comes not from treatment of the symptoms (the memories, the bad feelings, and so on) or underlying fears but by the acceptance of an alternative posture toward the world.[15] Such an alternative posture is provided by St. John of the Cross in his narrative of the journey of the soul.

The Dark Night of the Soul

St. John of the Cross, a sixteenth-century Spanish Carmelite priest and poet, set out to describe the soul's journey toward mystical union with God. It is ironic in such a secular time as ours — when so much of traditional faith has been destroyed by war, genocide, and the threat of nuclear annihilation, when God has been experienced primarily as absence (*Deus absconditus*) — that a quaint-sounding, four-hundred-year-old devotional manual on mystical union with God can provide a narrative clue to understanding contemporary experience. But strange as it may sound, such is indeed the case. In fact, it is difficult to understand the experience of Vietnam veterans in all its depth and fullness without reference to this narrative or others similar to it. Even if one no longer believes in God and therefore cannot use God-language to describe one's contemporary experience, John's poetic grasp of the dark night still rings true as an accurate portrayal of the inner life of combat vets and other survivors of twentieth-century devastation. As helpful as they are, even Conrad's understanding of the heart of darkness and Kristeva's exploration of abjection do not encompass the full experience as portrayed by this sixteenth-century Spanish mystic.

John of the Cross's most famous work, the *Dark Night of the Soul*, forms the fourth and final part of a larger work, the *Ascent of Mount Carmel*. This is a classic statement of apophatic, kenotic theology, the *via negativa*, a journey to

God that requires emptying or purging ourselves of every image, sensory perception, or affective attachment that is not God. The journey is not of our own making. We do not decide to embark on this journey, for it is "horrible and awful to the spirit" (*Dark Night* 1.8.2). It is God who brings us to this journey, and all our attempts to avoid it or delay it or take an alternative journey are in fact fruitless. Although the overall journey moves symbolically from twilight into midnight and then gradually emerges into a new dawn, the dark night is not experienced in neat, separate stages. The various movements overlap, combine, and transpose with one another as the journey gradually unfolds. Combat soldiers actually began the journey during the war itself, but because every thought and feeling that does not contribute to survival actually lessens the chances of survival in a combat zone, recognition of the journey was suppressed, either by an act of will or by alcohol and other drugs. It was only after their return from the war that vets were forced to come to terms with various dimensions of the dark night.

Constance FitzGerald, O.C.D., a most perceptive contemporary interpreter of John of the Cross, describes the dark night as first and foremost an experience of impasse. "There is no way out of, no way around, no rational escape from, what imprisons one, no possibilities in the situation.... The whole life situation suffers a depletion, has the word *limits* written upon it."[16] In another work, *Living Flame of Love*, written at the same time he was finishing the *Ascent of Mount Carmel*, John of the Cross cites Lamentations 3:1–9 as proof that the prophet Jeremiah understood God as the adversary who imposes such limits. Darkness, impasse, wounds, premature aging, imprisonment, powerlessness — every possible dimension of suffering, including turning a deaf ear, is at the hands of God:

> I am one who has seen affliction under the rod of God's wrath; he has driven and brought me into darkness without any light.... He has made my flesh and my skin waste away, and broken my bones; he has

besieged and enveloped me with bitterness and tribu-
lation; he has made me sit in darkness like the dead
of long ago. He has walled me about so that I cannot escape; he has put heavy chains on me; though I
call and cry for help, he shuts out my prayers; he has
blocked my ways with hewn stones, he has made my
paths crooked. (NRSV)

The dark night has many faces. They speak to us of
death although in reality they provide the occasion for
growth and new life. The signs or symptoms of this journey sound like a litany of the laments voiced by vets: life
loses its savor; there is a sense of deadness and distaste;
confusion replaces certainty; communication breaks down;
capacity for intimacy is lost; one experiences terrible lone-
liness yet desires only solitude; one feels exhausted and
unable to concentrate for long on anything; one is haunted
by disappointment, disillusionment, loss of meaning and
self-worth, a sense of failure and shame, a feeling of abandonment and betrayal; and above all one is possessed by
the overwhelming sense of powerlessness to change anything. "Since God puts a soul in this dark night in order to
dry up and purge its sensory appetite, [God] does not allow it to find sweetness or delight in anything" (*Dark Night*
1.9.2).

The Vietnam veteran Emmett in the novel and film *In
Country* is imprisoned in such an impasse. Life no longer
has any taste or meaning for him. He lives in a daze,
alternating between staring fixedly at the television and
digging yet another foxhole in his backyard. When his
niece Sam finally succeeds in drawing him out, Emmett explains: "There's something wrong with me. I'm damaged.
It's like something in the center of my heart is gone and
I can't get it back. You know when you cut down a tree
sometimes and it's diseased in the middle?"[17]

Face-to-face with darkness, the vet has four choices: to
attack, to flee, to give up, or to embrace the night. Marilyn's father has chosen the first three. He still dreams of the

day when he can vindicate his honor. A scapegoat himself, he also practices scapegoating, for he blames the antiwar movement, the press, the government, and the military for not allowing the grunts to win. Yet deep within he carries another knowledge — of human limits, of evil, of guilt and shame — from which he hides. Until he confronts that knowledge, he cannot regain his passion for life. And so he has succumbed to "the most dangerous temptation, [which] is to give up, to quit, to surrender to cynicism and despair, in the face of the disappointment, disenchantment, hopelessness, and loss of meaning that encompasses" him.[18] Marilyn signed up for my class because she realized at some level that her father's suffering was hers as well and that if her father could not face the night, she would have to face it for both of them.

To embrace the night is fearful and dangerous because it requires the relinquishment of former ways of thinking and feeling, former patterns of behavior, former relationships of support, former systems of meaning. "What the sorrowful soul feels most in this condition," writes John, "is that God has abandoned it, and, in His abhorrence of it, has flung it into darkness" (*Dark Night* 2.6.2). Dorothee Soelle comments on this experience: "All extreme suffering evokes the experience of being forsaken by God. In the depth of suffering people see themselves as abandoned and forsaken by everyone. That which gave life its meaning has become empty and void: it turned out to be an error, an illusion that is shattered, a guilt that cannot be rectified, a void. The paths that lead to this experience of nothingness are diverse, but the experience of annihilation that occurs is the same."[19] Some vets have been overwhelmed by the darkness and have chosen suicide rather than the agony of abandonment.

For John this agony is part of the path to God, the necessary purgation of every other appetite and affection, every other commitment and goal that stands in the way of our union with God. John's assumption is that all human beings are rooted and grounded in God's love, and nothing but God can satisfy our deepest hungers. This fundamental premise echoes Augustine, who wrote, "Thou hast made us for Thyself, and our hearts are restless until they find their rest in Thee."

The difficulty arises from the various commitments, attachments, appetites, and desires that prevent us from discovering this reality. These serve as substitute gods, idols that cannot satisfy but that impede integration and wholeness. The path to this "great awakening," as John calls it, carries us on a journey through the agony of purgation. This painful but necessary journey — a journey to liberation through dis-illusionment — brings death to false gods, leaving us "alone, lost, and hurt."[20] Only when we have exhausted all other possibilities, when we have put our trust in other gods and they have failed, are we able to understand that nothing — no thing — is God, and nothing else but God brings fulfillment and peace. At that point and only at that point — when life seems dead, when all meaning is lost, when all hope of help from another source is dashed — are we open to experience newness from God.

This classical, orthodox Christian theology may sound strange to modern ears, but Bill Mahedy, cofounder of the nationwide storefront vet centers sponsored by the Veterans Administration, operates out of this framework. So do those vet center directors and counselors whom Mahedy has influenced, in spite of the official link between these centers and the U.S. government. Another widely successful ministry for vets, Point Man International, also operates essentially from this perspective, using contemporary evangelical language rather than that of sixteenth-century mysticism.

It is not necessary to be a Christian or even to believe in God to emerge with new hope on the other side of the dark night. In his therapeutic work with vets, the agnostic psychiatrist Arthur Egendorf articulates a similar, but secular, version of this narrative, laced with concepts and terminology from the Buddhist experience of enlightenment. Egendorf agrees with Mahedy, vet center directors, and leaders of Point Man International that without an alternative narrative that takes account of dark-night experiences, holistic healing does not occur. Since the dominant cultural narrative, American Exceptionalism, has no place for the dark night, holistic ministries with vets require a different narrative that "fits" with the vets' experiences during and after the war.

Once we are brought to the dark night, whether by means of wartime combat or other deep losses, there is no assurance that we will make it through the night to a new dawn. Darkness is frightening, dangerous, fraught with uncertainty. Great courage and patience are required to face the darkness and wait for the dawn. And even if we complete the journey, we — like Jacob at the River Jabbok — will carry forever in our bodies and souls the marks of our nocturnal wrestling with God.

Revelation and the Struggles of the Dark Night

Successful navigation of the dark night depends upon one's willingness to fulfill four conditions: (1) to embrace the experience of impasse consciously, fully, and willingly; (2) to face squarely the human condition with all its limitations, capacity for evil, and existential powerlessness; (3) to relinquish the desire for control; and (4) to surrender freely to mystery, which leads us on a journey toward the margin of life, from which place solidarity with all humankind becomes a possibility.[21] These conditions are related to the steps in healing mentioned above: remembering, reexperiencing, confronting and reinterpreting. Together they describe the inner process by which vets receive revelation and struggle under its influence to reconfigure their lives.

In his classic treatment of this subject, H. Richard Niebuhr describes how we construct our life-stories and worldviews using "evil imaginations of the heart." Such stories and worldviews are forms of self-deception, "cover stories"[22] that have harmful consequences for persons and communities because they distort reality and mystify many of life's experiences. Revelation, says Niebuhr, is "that special occasion which provides us with an image by means of which all the occasions of personal and common life become intelligible."[23] The "special occasion" involves each of the steps and conditions mentioned above, by which the cover story is discarded in favor of a more adequate understanding of the human condition and its possibilities.

Arthur Egendorf provides an example; he describes it as a process of "waking up." Even though the substance of his description of the enlightenment experience differs from the content of the Christian narrative, phenomenologically the dynamics are similar to those described by Niebuhr's term "revelation." While working with the CIA in Saigon, Egendorf climbed up on the roof of a building with other Americans during a Vietcong night attack on parts of the city. As the others joked and laughed at the plight of victims caught in the firefight, an unusual repulsion shook him. They were laughing at human brutality and misery as if they themselves were immune to the same fate. At that moment Egendorf realized that "the struggle I had made the center of my life" — the search for security and acceptance — "was pointless and vain."[24] After his return to the United States he tried to forget the war, but that "special occasion" on the rooftop in Saigon haunted him. His book *Healing from the War* offers a gripping account of how, in a rap group, he embraced the impasse, faced human limitation, relinquished his desire for control, and surrendered to mystery. Under the influence of that rooftop revelation he probed Buddhist texts and, over a period of years, gradually succeeded in reinterpreting his life — and the whole human condition — by means of the image of "waking up."

Paradoxically, the dark night is the locus of revelation where new vision is possible. How ironic, that one sees only in darkness — that the clay feet of our idols and the evil imaginations of the heart that we use to create them are visible only when we encounter impasse.

In chapter 5 we discussed the demise of one idol, American Exceptionalism and the racism that accompanies it. Now let us look briefly at the fatal wounds inflicted by two other forms of self-deception during the vets' dark night. These are the cover stories of cultural religion and macho masculinity.

Cultural religion has served as handmaiden to Americanism, taking institutional expression in the military chaplaincy.[25] Although in their own minds many chaplains make a clear distinction between God and country, the institution that they serve blends the two. They are assigned to the military as chaplains by their religious bodies, and they hold the rank of military officers. Bill Mahedy remarked in a conversation that although he and others ripped their officer insignias from their uniforms, in the eyes of soldiers the two identities were merged. Indeed, the motto of the Army Chaplain Corps is *Pro Deo et Patria* (for God and country); the chaplain is inseparable from the "green machine" whose purpose is killing; and there is "no perceived disjunction between the intention of God and the American cause."[26]

Lifton notes that both psychiatrists and chaplains regarded their professions in such narrow "technicist" terms that their role in Vietnam degenerated into that of helping men adjust to committing war crimes. The vets whom he interviewed "were trying to say that the only thing worse than being ordered by military authorities to participate in absurd evil is to have that evil rationalized and justified by guardians of the spirit."[27] Most of the chaplains I have interviewed give evidence of a deep malaise that derives from the ambiguity of their structural position. They remember their combat duty as the most important form of ministry they have ever exercised. At the same time they recognize that many soldiers viewed them as morale officers supporting "a counterfeit universe in which all-pervasive, spiritually-reinforced inner corruption [became] the price of survival."[28]

In short, the chaplaincy as an institution supports the cover story of Americanism and therefore contributes to the faith crisis that leads to the dark night. Because vets have been inoculated by a distorted view of the Jewish or Christian message, they are not very open to embracing an authentic, alternative religious narrative. As long as the current institutional linkage between the chaplaincy and the military remains unchanged and as long as the churches and seminaries where chaplains are trained blend Christian faith with Americanism, the religious bodies that assign chaplains to the armed forces will continue to participate in the maintenance of the cover story. When revelation comes to vets, it will inevitably alienate them from religious narratives and make more difficult their task of reinterpretation.

Macho masculinity may prove even more difficult for vets to reinterpret. During the buildup for Desert Storm, I interviewed a colonel responsible for deploying chaplains to all those medical facilities where the American wounded would be sent. Military strategists were preparing for up to one hundred thousand American casualties. This colonel had bitter memories of the impossible situation his men had faced in Vietnam, yet he embodied the "spirit of the grunt." He proudly reported how even now at midlife he could outrun most eighteen-year-old recruits. As a specialist in pastoral care and counseling, he was thoroughly aware of his feelings and reported how angry he was with President Bush for provoking a showdown with Saddam Hussein. "This war's about presidential ego and national oil supplies, not human rights and national sovereignty. We have no business there!" At the same time he was envious of those who would go to the front lines. "If they would let me, I'd go in a minute, even though I think it is suicidal. It's so exciting. Every nerve ending in your whole body tingles with anticipation. Read Bill Broyles's article in *Esquire*, 'Why Men Love War.' He says it all."

Even the subtitle of Broyles's article says it all: "The Awesome Beauty, the Haunting Romance, of the Timeless Nightmare." War calls upon the very best in the human soul: adventure, courage, sacrifice, dedication, loyalty, comradeship (which is "the only utopian experience most of us every have").[29] At the same time it brings out the very worst. Broyles recounts one battle in which his unit slaughtered a large number of North Vietnamese Army troops. The next morning as they were cleaning up the bodies he noticed a beatific smile on the face of his commanding officer. Broyles returned the expression. "That was another of the times I stood on the edge of my humanity, looked into the pit, and loved what I saw there.... To give the devil his due,... [war is] an affair of great and seductive beauty."[30]

What Broyles and this colonel have missed is the underlying need for machismo that fuels the love of war and their version of masculinity. This need derives from a deep sense of personal unworthiness and the belief that by becoming a hero one's self-worth can be earned. In an interview with a vet who teaches occasional university courses on the war, I asked if he ever uses the film *Born on the Fourth of July* in his classes. "Never!" he snapped. "Ron Kovic didn't learn the most important thing in Vietnam!" Then he explained. "Remember that scene in the high school gym? The state wrestling championship or something like that. And his mother was yelling her head off for him. His opponent pinned him to the mat, and at that moment he looked up into the stands at his mother. She turned her head in shame. Right after that he signed up for the marines to prove himself. Even though he turned against the war after his injury, he still had to play the hero — this time an antiwar hero — at the Republican Convention. Kovic still doesn't get it. It's the hero thing that does us in."

The movie *Coming Home* illustrates this point. Bob went to Vietnam because, as he says, "I wanted to be a hero. I wanted to go out and kill for my country." When he returns, he confesses in tears to his wife, "I have killed for my country and I don't feel good about it." The movie ends with one final but futile gesture of heroism: Bob carefully removes his dress uniform, folds it neatly, and places it on the lifeguard stand. Then he plunges into the ocean to end his life.

Revelation "makes our past intelligible," wrote Niebuhr. "Through it we understand what we remember, remember what we have forgotten and appropriate as our own past much that seemed alien to us."[31] Those who persist on their journey through the dark night discern the shadow side of "the spirit of the grunt." They discover the destructiveness of the macho cover story, the "hero thing," and the self-doubt that fuels it. "Eventually [they] dissolve even the belief that [they] are unworthy."[32]

At this point they are approaching the dawn and the new communal responsibilities that await them. These duties include the contribution of their revelation to the national task of narrative reconstruction. Because our personal narratives are shaped by and dependent upon corporate narratives — we are never atomistic individuals but always persons in community — any healing process requires corporate as well as personal re-storying. This is the subject of the final chapter.

Chapter Seven

Hope in a Time of Impasse

> In a way we are all recovering Vietnam veterans.
> —Joel Brende and Erwin Parson,
> *Vietnam Veterans: The Road to Recovery*

The Shattered American Dream

In the introduction I described vision gridlock at the national level. Gridlock signals the loss of a corporate narrative appropriate to our time in history. The succeeding chapters have explored how the American Dream was shattered for many Vietnam veterans, leaving them — and the nation — without clear purpose or direction. This chapter explores various "readings" of our sociohistorical context that attempt to make sense of our current plight and concludes with a reflection on the nourishment of hope in a period of impasse. This is a first step in the re-storying process that lies before us as a nation.

There is little doubt that we as a people are demoralized today. Shortly after the 1992 election a friend of mine remarked: "Bill Clinton's primary task is to deal with our growing national anxiety. If he can't find a cure for our fears, he'll be a one-term president."[1] Whether the cause be immigration, anticipated job-loss due to the North American Free Trade Agreement, the disintegration of our public schools, inner-city violence, or one of the many other challenges that face us today, the level of fear continues to rise. The request for use of the National Guard to police the streets of the nation's capital would have been unthinkable in an earlier period. Fear arises because we have lost our sense of destiny. We recognize the signs of a crumbling culture, but we lack any blueprint for constructing an alternative future because we no longer have what Latin American theologians call a *proyecto histórico* (historical project).

Richard Slotkin has observed that "in a demoralized community, the effective connection between perception, belief, and action is broken or confounded. No single course of action recommends itself as a way out of the impasse, although inaction also seems intolerable. Language and imagination seem unequal to the tasks of defining the problem, expressing the causes of disaffection, or conceiving a desirable resolution of the crisis."[2] This is an apt description of our current situation. Anxiety, frustration, anger, and fear mingle with grief for that which has been lost.

Figure 7 pictures three distinct stages of cultural grieving that may be discerned in times of collective loss.[3] Although these stages are conceptually distinct, they are not chronologically discrete. They overlap and interpenetrate. Some people may be stuck in an earlier stage while the larger culture moves on to a later stage. The Reagan-Bush years were characterized by a nostalgic, reactive stance; Clinton appears to possess the will to move in the direction of recovery, but his administration's programs are encountering great resistance from both political parties because they lack any clear and persuasive vision that would draw us into an alternative future.

In light of our current malaise, let us examine several different "readings" of our situation, with particular attention to their attitudinal and behavioral scenarios. The major criterion in my assessment of these readings is their capacity to re-story the national narrative, taking full account of veterans' experiences of darkness.

Figure 7
Stages of Cultural Grieving

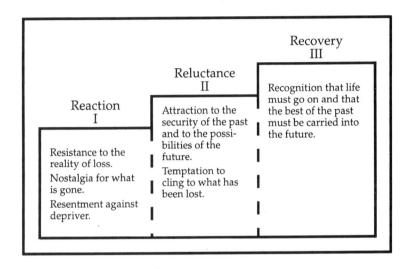

The Religious Right:
Relinking God and Country

Today the religious right is regarded as a powerful, well-organized, grassroots movement capable of controlling the platform of the Republican Party and shaping the terms of national debate. In spite of this image, the religious right is really a loosely organized, fluid movement comprised of diverse groups — evangelical and fundamentalist Protestants and conservative Roman Catholics — depending upon the issues in question. This movement's rise to political prominence is a rather recent phenomenon with roots in at least four aspects of the social revolution of the 1960s and early 1970s: the 1961 Supreme Court ban on school prayer, forced integration of the schools, the anti–Vietnam War movement, and the sexual revolution (symbolized by the 1973 Supreme Court *Roe v. Wade* decision on abortion rights). Taken together, these four developments place under siege the major institutions that supported a traditional worldview: family, religion, school, and nation.

The big switch to political activism by the religious right came with its use of television in the early 1970s. At that time television stations began charging for religious broadcasting. While the mainline churches refused to enter the market, the conservatives entered big, raising vast sums of money on television. At the same time, evangelists such as Jerry Falwell, Jim Robison, Pat Robertson, and Jim Bakker began adding political commentaries to their television programs. While the Vietnam War and the Watergate scandal pushed the religious left toward liberation theology, the right was preparing itself organizationally to enter the political arena in defense of a "strong America" and a return to traditional morality. In 1976, Jerry Falwell gained considerable publicity for his "I Love America" rallies held on the steps of state capitols. In 1979 the Moral Majority was established with Falwell as its president and with backing from people like Paul Weyrich, Richard Viguerie, and Howard Phillips of the political new right, who were seeking an alliance with religion to broaden their appeal. The new religious right and the new political right united around issues of anticommunism, capitalism, patriotism, prayer, Bible reading, the teaching of creation science, "family values," gender roles, the media, crime and violence, homosexuality, abortion, and pornography. Since America, according to the right, is God's chosen standard-bearer of freedom in the world, American decline must be due to national faithlessness. The Moral Majority and other groups of the religious right are credited with the Reagan victory at the polls in 1980.

Undergirding the worldview of the religious right is a retribution theology similar to that of the Deuteronomist editor of the Old Testament. Obedience to God is rewarded with national blessings; disobedience is punished with national decline. Thus these groups blur distinctions between nation and church. The religious right has been accused of authoritarian dogmatism, substituting revelation for reason in public debate, and attempting to create a theocracy ("Christian America"). The right has an absolutist tone, but these charges do not apply uniformly to the great diversity of religious groups on the right. The one belief they do share is that American decline is first and foremost a *moral* decline, with repercussions in every area of public and private life. This decline is due, they believe, to the takeover of public institutions — especially the courts, the schools, Hollywood, and the media — by a false religion: secular humanism. The argument can be summarized as follows. American institutions have become in fact antireligious. Respect for individual rights and religious pluralism have combined with the humanistic assumptions of the Enlightenment (supreme trust in reason, science, and technology; disdain of religion as an outdated form of superstition; the desire for control over human destiny; a doctrine of progress; the absence of any transcendent reference or standards) and more recent claims that reality itself is humanly constructed and therefore relative. This antireligious slant creates an ethical vacuum.

The ban on prayer and Bible reading in public schools illustrates this point. Those who favor the ban claim that public institutions should be neutral in matters of religion. This is the meaning of the "no-establishment" clause of the First Amendment, they say. Not so, says the religious right. Neutrality is not possible: the schools foster either a respect and appreciation for religion or a neglect and disrespect of religion. The freedom of religion clause of the First Amendment balances the no-establishment clause. Historically, American institutions have been respectful and appreciative of religion. Recent Supreme Court decisions, however, have reversed this age-old status of religion in American life.

In recent years liberals have come to appreciate the strength of this position. Even some of the fiercest opponents of the religious right, like Norman Lear, have

changed their views on the place of religion in school curricula. In 1991 Lear, a television producer and the head of
People for the American Way — a secularist, left-of-center
group — addressed a meeting of the largest professional
association of teachers of religion, the American Academy
of Religion (AAR). He acknowledged that the removal of
religion from education borders on censorship and that
this has been harmful for the teaching of history and an
understanding of what motivates human behavior. One
of the most active sections of the AAR is devoted to the
development of public school curricula and methods for
teaching "about" religion that the courts will not strike
down. This section of the AAR recognizes that the neglect
of religion in school curricula distorts history and neglects
wisdom from the past, thus contributing to a superficial
preoccupation with the contemporaneous, a "flattening" of
historical memory.

Richard John Neuhaus, a civil rights and antiwar activist turned neoconservative, has provided the most articulate defense of the new right's position on religion.
Building on the theoretical work of classical sociologist
Emile Durkheim, Neuhaus notes that societies are held
together by a core of sacred beliefs and values. "The public square [Neuhaus's term for public institutions] will
not and cannot remain naked." All societies are by the
very nature of things religious, because "religion is the
morality-bearing part of culture." "What is called neutrality toward religion is an invitation for a substitute
religion." The public square will be clothed either with
some historic religion or with some ersatz religion like
secular humanism. Although Neuhaus criticizes the theo-
cratic, antidemocratic tendencies of the religious right, he
nevertheless concurs with their diagnosis that national
decline is due to the takeover by secular humanism. "American democracy is in the midst of a legitimation crisis." The
task of religion is "to help reconstruct a 'sacred canopy' for
the American experiment," to provide "a meaning and a
purpose" to the national narrative.[4] In the United States,

the Judeo-Christian tradition is the only religious tradition that can viably serve the nation in this manner.

Neither Neuhaus nor the TV evangelists who nourish the religious right have understood the dark night experience of the Vietnam generation. Because they do not recognize the collective American shadow, their speeches and writings have a triumphalistic tone that ignores the experiences of disillusionment of the 1960s and 1970s. For them, American Exceptionalism is still alive and well, even if others have defected. Several neoconservative religious intellectuals, including Neuhaus, Michael Novak, Peter Berger, George Weigel, and the evangelical Carl F. H. Henry, have added their influence to a revival of American Exceptionalism. By their leadership in the Institute on Religion and Democracy (IRD), founded in 1981 and called by some "the department of religion" of the Reagan presidency,[5] they have supported a revisionist interpretation of Vietnam and its meaning for America. In a manifesto entitled "Christianity and Democracy," the IRD declares a fundamental theological premise: "America has a peculiar place in God's promises and purposes."[6] When one starts from that premise, God's cause and the nation's fortunes are joined, religion is reduced to its utilitarian role of serving national "interests," and Christian opposition to misuse of American power is blunted. IRD support for the Reagan administration's misuse of power in Central America illustrates this point.

George M. Marsden, a scholar of Fundamentalism in America, takes issue with the religious right and neoconservatives like those linked to the IRD. Too close a linkage between religion and "the public square" can lead to compromises of religion itself, so that secularism is strengthened by the inner corruption of official religion. "The naked public square could be a symbol of what is *right* about American tradition rather than of what is wrong."[7] The intimate embrace of the Reagan presidency by the religious right and the IRD supports Marsden's view.

Resident Aliens:
Unlinking God and Country

Stanley Hauerwas and William Willimon concur with
the diagnosis of secularism and moral decline, but their
agenda calls for a radical break between the Christian
story and the national story. For them, the primary reality
the church in the United States today faces is its margin-
alization from the center of cultural influence. The major
institutions of society are independent of religion, operat-
ing according to their own autonomous, secular principles.
Business is controlled by profits, government by national
interest, the media by the market, and education by agnostic positivism. Religion has been relegated to private
life, and former moral standards have become matters of
personal choice. Thus, society is no longer a prop for the
church. The era of American Christian Constantinianism
has ended.

This is not a cause for grief but for celebration, argue
Hauerwas and Willimon, because Christians are now free
for a new kind of adventure as a colony of resident aliens.
Christians live in a hostile culture that does not share many
of the presuppositions of their faith. In fact, the dominant
worldview upon which American society is based — democracy, progress, individualism — undermines the very
concept of a corporate story:

> The primary entity of democracy is the individual, the
> individual for whom society exists mainly to assist
> assertions of individuality. Society is formed to sup-
> ply our needs, no matter the content of those needs.
> Rather than helping us to judge our needs, to have
> the right needs which we exercise in right ways, our
> society becomes a vast supermarket of desire under
> the assumption we can defer eternally the question of
> what needs are worth having and on what basis right
> choices are made. What we call "freedom" becomes
> the tyranny of our own desires.[8]

Under these circumstances the self shrinks instead of growing.

The task of the church today in the United States is not to transform the world; liberal Christianity tried that and failed, becoming corrupted by the world. Today the task of the church is merely to be the church. "We serve the world by showing it something that it is not, namely, a place where God is forming a family out of strangers."[9]

There are three models of the church: the *activist* church (which seeks to build a better society by humanizing the laws and institutions of society); the *conversionist* church (which works only for inward change in individuals and therefore has no social ethic or social structure of its own to offer the world); and the *confessing* church. The confessing church "moves from the activist church's acceptance of the culture with a few qualifications, to rejection of the culture with a few exceptions."[10]

Only a confessing church with the true story can confront American culture with its false story. The war in Vietnam "was not just a national goof, an unfortunate mistake, but rather derived from the deepest and most cherished American beliefs about ourselves. We really do want to run the world, to set things right, to spread democracy and freedom everywhere. We really want to believe . . . that America is different from other nations . . . [that] we do not act out of self-interest but out of ideals."[11] Nothing short of a radical *unlinking* of the Christian story from the American story will suffice to clarify the true nature of each narrative.

If theocracy is the dominant temptation of the religious right, Hauerwas and Willimon appear to embrace the opposite temptation, namely, withdrawal and social irresponsibility. This impression is reinforced by their thorough pacifism as well as their reluctance to articulate a social ethic or a national story that would encourage Christian citizenship in a religiously pluralistic society. Their preoccupation with the church ignores the presence of God in society, what Tillich called "the structure of grace in history." On the other hand, their withdrawal from social engagement amounts to what Harvey Cox has called "leaving it to the snake." The major Christian tradition understands that discipleship includes citizenship as one means of caring for neighbor. If, in John Calvin's sense, government is provided by God to restrain evil and promote good, then Christian welfare is tied to national welfare too. The exiles were told to seek the welfare of Babylon. Shouldn't Christians do the same in secular America?

Exile: A Religious Narrative
for Church and Nation

For over a decade now Walter Brueggemann has been mining the texts of the exilic and postexilic period. He is convinced that the biblical metaphor of exile is the most appropriate "dynamic analogy" for understanding the contemporary plight of all areas of life in the United States, whether economic, political, cultural, or religious.[12]

Until recently, Christian biblical scholars have neglected the postexilic period after the fall of Jerusalem in 587 B.C.E., forgetting that the prophets of this era rescued Jewish faith from destruction. By creatively reworking the tradition in light of the new situation, they gave birth to the Judaism of the synagogue. Christian scholarly neglect of this period is due not only to the dominant "Wellhausian hypothesis," which regarded this period as one of degeneration, not worthy of attention; it is due also to the fact that the church has considered itself a part of the establishment in "the American century." Leaders of the church — as chaplains to the rulers — saw their prophetic task to be that of influencing policy rather than consoling the dispossessed.

In 587 B.C.E. the Babylonians destroyed Jerusalem and with it the two pillars of religious faith and national identity, the temple and the Davidic dynasty. Since the temple was God's habitation in Israel and the king God's representative among the people, their loss meant the death of the God they had known. Was God no longer faithful to the covenant? Or was God powerless to save? The death of God meant the demise of their known world.

Thus the exile was not just geographical displacement. More traumatic was the loss of personal and corporate identity, the destruction of meaning and purpose in life. For the survivors then — just as for the survivors of Dachau and Auschwitz, Hiroshima and Phnom Penh, and the homeless vets with a "one-thousand-yard stare" wandering aimlessly on the streets of our cities — exile is different from captivity. When released, captives can return home. But once one's identity and structure of meaning are destroyed, "home" no longer exists. Instead, one is left powerless, with only shattered dreams, nostalgic wistfulness, and vengeful rage. Psalm 137, like a *Rambo* film, plays on these classic exilic themes of abandonment, rage, and vengeful violence: "Happy shall they be who take your little ones and dash them against the rock!" (Psalm 37:9).

Like ancient Israel's, our exile is both religious and cultural. We are experiencing the unraveling of our cultural story while at the same time religion is being marginalized by pluralism and secularization. And even though this disestablishment of dominant groups raises hopes of emancipation for women and people of color, only modest gains by the latter groups are likely in a shrinking economy.

The task of prophecy in times of exile is to help the community grieve over what has been lost, relinquish the past that will never return, and reinterpret the communal narrative for a new context in history. Without merging or radically separating religion from culture, Brueggemann mines a rich metaphor from one religious tradition in the hope that it might prove useful for interpreting the experiences even of those who do not share that tradition.

The Good Society:
Creating a Secular, Pluralistic Narrative

While the religious right is the most vocal movement protesting American decline, it is not alone. Academicians
have wrestled with underlying causes of this decline. Perhaps the best-known group of scholars working in this
area is the team of philosophers and social scientists led
by Berkeley sociologist Robert Bellah. Their two jointly authored studies, *Habits of the Heart* and *The Good Society*,[13]
have received wide acclaim. The more technical analysis of
team member William M. Sullivan, entitled *Reconstructing
Public Philosophy*,[14] underlies both the diagnosis of decline
and the prescription for renewal provided in the two team
studies.

The Bellah team concurs with Durkheim's thesis that
societies are held together by a common, almost sacred,
core of beliefs and values that gives meaning and purpose to corporate life. Historically, the United States has
maintained two conflicting views: one elevates individual
freedom and choice above every other value, while the
other raises justice and the common good above private,
individual good. These two conflicting views of life were
blended into a marriage of convenience until recently, with
individualism (enshrined in the Constitution, the economy,
and the American frontier spirit) being held in check by a
public ethos shaped by the Judeo-Christian heritage and
the republican traditions of classical Greece and Rome.

Applying the terminology of Neuhaus and a basic thesis of the religious right to this analysis, we can say that the
public square in the United States has never been naked.
From the earliest days of the American republic, when
the philosophic liberalism of John Locke eclipsed civic re-
publicanism in the Federalist Constitution of 1787, a form
of secular humanism has dominated national life. According to liberalism, "individuality exists outside of or prior
to social relationships."[15] Society is the result of a social
contract among atomistic individuals, a necessary evil to

assist in the pursuit of private interests. Thus, the purpose of government is negative: to prevent harm by serving as an umpire balancing the interests of competing individuals. Since the source of value lies in individual preference and will, value is dissolved into power and politics into an arena for clashing interests. "In its extreme forms, [liberalism] denies meaning and value to even the notion of common purpose, or politics in its classic sense."[16]

As long as the United States had a frontier with vast untapped resources, the inherent contradictions between liberalism and the common good were masked by economic growth and social progress. Everyone benefited to some degree. These conditions no longer exist today. Instead, we face limits on every front: declining political and military power overseas, greater economic competition from abroad, environmental restraints and declining natural resources. The Reagan years illustrate how radically the situation has changed from a win-win to a win-lose position. A zero-sum game now operates, where the gains of some require losses from others. At the same time, religious pluralism, increasing secularization, and the breakdown of community and family life have accentuated the split between public and private life. Now the religious and civil ethos that formerly restrained excessive individualism is too weak to function in this manner. As a result, individualism has turned in upon itself, like a snake devouring its own tail. Having no external standards from religious traditions or from contemporary society by which to judge what is good and right, people are left with only their own visceral urges as guides. This situation is reflected in the entertainment industry, where the menu is dominated by sex, violence, and other visceral titillations.

Other scholars from differing ideological perspectives support this critique of liberalism. Sullivan examines the work of three writers — Fred Hirsch (*Social Limits to Growth*), Daniel Bell (*The Cultural Contradictions of Capitalism*), and Robert Heilbroner (*Business Civilization in Decline*)[17] — and notes that all three "portray the liberal world as coming unstuck as the workings of its basic institutions generate effects destructive of the natural and social environment they depend upon for their survival. The whole liberal construction of an analytic science, an individualistic motivation, and an instrumental, utilitarian politics, which had seemed a complete and objectively secured — almost self-evident — view of human affairs, is now at sea."[18] *The Good Society*, one of the texts written by the team led by Robert Bellah, documents how a basic premise of individualism — the principle of immediate, private interest-maximization — has become institutionalized in American life in such a way that the "tyranny of the market" is "strip-mining" cooperation and trust from all institutions, including government, business, education, religion, and the family.[19] Things are falling apart because individualism provides no moral guide, only a jungle of competing private interests.

Ronald Thiemann, dean of the Harvard Divinity School, believes that the major task of social ethics in America today is the re-creation of the possibility of public discourse, which has disintegrated under the impact of pluralistic individualism. We have "lost a living sense of citizenship," says Thiemann, because "we lack the one thing needful for genuine moral discussion — a common understanding of the *telos* of human existence."[20]

The Bellah team thus shares with the religious right and many others a concern for the loss of moral purpose in the United States, even while differing in its understanding of the causes of moral decline. Because the Bellah team values pluralism and religious freedom and does not wish to see a single religious perspective imposed on the nation, it is concerned not about removing secular humanism from the public square but rather about exchanging one form of humanism for another. For the team's members, the only way to arrest American decline is to replace Lockean individualism with a concept of the good society, a "new ethic of equity and cooperation" derived by reasoned debate and sustained by democratic consensus.[21]

The Bellah team does not flesh out the major components of a good society, perhaps because its members believe this should be done through a process of dialogue among various sectors of society. They do call for the recreation of community life where such dialogue and debate can take place. The Good Society Project of the Center for Ethics and Social Policy of the Graduate Theological Union in Berkeley carries forward their contribution to this discussion.

The good-society proposal suffers from the same major weakness that plagues all secular ethics, namely, the absence of a mythopoetic narrative with deep affective resonance. Although incisive in its analysis of the Enlightenment forces that have marginalized religious narratives, and appropriately wary of any attempt to reimpose the hegemony of any single religious narrative, the good-society proposal relies upon the instruments of the Enlightenment (reason and goodwill) to escape the impasse created by goals of that eighteenth-century movement. Perhaps this is why Ronald Thiemann suggests an alternative: the vigorous mining and recovery of our religious traditions and more active engagement by religious communities in the pluralistic public discussion of the common good. Only in this manner, Thiemann believes, can we avoid the twin dangers of religious hegemony and moral relativism.[22]

Night Vision and the Revival of Hope

In spite of their conflicting interpretations of the sociohistorical situation, each of these "readings" contributes to an understanding of our contemporary plight. The Enlightenment, which sought freedom from religious dogmatism and clerical abuse of power, gave birth to its own nemesis. By crediting humans with godlike powers of control, the new "Science of Man" removed the restraints on human desire and turned vice (Promethean hubris) into virtue.

Secular humanism, especially in the form of Lockean individualism, has introduced a cancerous narcissism into the organs of our cultural and institutional life. No foreign enemy has conquered us, yet we feel like exiles within our own country. Something — we can't always say quite what — has been lost. Like Brer Rabbit with the tar baby, the more we flail at our problems, the more immobilized we become. In spite of Herculean efforts to shape public policy and transform society over the past fifty years, the churches appear captive to the culture and powerless to challenge the prevailing spirit of the age. It is as if we as a nation, along with much of humanity, are undergoing not only exile but also a massive "dark night of the world."[23]

Are we at the end of an era, not merely the end of "the American century"? If after only seventy years the demise of communism in the member nations of the former Soviet Union brings such upheaval, we shudder to think of the magnitude of the changes that await us if the foundations of the "modern era" crumble beneath us. Religious communities in our time must help us overcome our fear, embrace this communal dark night, and open ourselves to receive a different dream.

The dark night means impasse. Things fall apart. Old solutions no longer work; instead, old solutions provoke new problems. Like a giant neon sign flashing "LIMITS! LIMITS!" impasse announces "NO!" to the old dream. Nothing in the repertoire of modern society — reason, science, technology, advanced degrees in management and organizational development — appears capable of putting things back on track. We can't even agree on what is wrong, and we see no light at the end of the tunnel. "There seems no possibility of movement backward or forward but only imprisonment, lack of vision, and failure of imagination."[24]

The dark night brings confusion. A dryness pervades our life together, leaving us empty and weak, devoid of creative energy. Failure undermines our sense of self-worth. We feel isolated, abandoned, vulnerable. Our compassion for the old, the weak, the sick, and the oppressed — what Hubert Humphrey called the mark of a civilized society — atrophies, lest we render ourselves more vulnerable. We become cautious, fearful of risk, protecting what we have. Each act of senseless violence drives us farther into our protective enclaves.

The dark night robs us of our power. No longer do we feel in control. We lose the ability to see, to know, and to act. We feel helpless, at the mercy of forces we cannot discern or understand. Americans are not educated for darkness. We are "the officially optimistic society,"[25] with little sense of limits or of the tragic. Therefore, the temptation is avoidance, denial, flight.

But limits, confusion, and loss of power are only the initial experiences of darkness. Paradoxically, hope is born in the night, and only in the night. Optimism, not despair, is the enemy of hope. Optimism blinds us to the shadow side of life. Optimism wears a forced smile, represses intuitive danger signals, and projects its own evil onto others. Optimism is a lie that denies the truth and therefore prevents necessary change. Hope, then, arises not amid optimism but amid the ruins of crumbled dreams.

A middle-aged pastor commented on how hope arose for him in the dark night following his divorce:

> Broken. That's how I would describe it. For several years I had a vague feeling all was not right between us, but I kept a stiff upper lip because I was afraid to open up. When she left me, I felt broken, ... abandoned, ... and betrayed! I went through hell for a while, but you know, it was the best thing my wife could have done for me — not that she was trying to do me any favors at that time. But it was just what I needed. Forced to face my failure, I entered into a dark and lonely period. But how creative! When I vented my anger on God, I felt drawn by God deeper into the darkness. Then I realized there was no turning back. Like Jacob I had to wrestle with God all night long.

That's when I discovered a special verse from Psalm 88 in the New American Bible: "My only friend is Darkness." Imagine! Darkness can be a *friend!* I began to see things — things about myself, about life, and about God — that had been hidden from me before. It took a long time — lots of therapy and hard, angry prayer — but I'm a different person now. I'm no longer driven. I feel at home with myself, and I've gained a new freedom. I still carry the pain, but now I no longer have to fake it. Now what you see is what you get. I'm *authentic.* And that's a huge relief!"

In like manner, impasse can be the source of hope and freedom for us as a nation. Impasse is a necessary stage in every major historical transition, for without impasse we would continue on our accustomed way, oblivious to the disintegration around us. In this sense impasse is a *gift* that signals the opening of new possibilities, a gift that can relieve us of the burden of a distorted national dream.

The task today for religious communities in the United States is to help the nation *redefine our situation.* Redefinition of the situation may occur at various levels and may change the way we perceive and live. At the personal level, for example, the director of chaplaincy at a large hospital reports that nurses working in an oncology ward burn out earlier and more frequently than nurses working in a hospice program. He attributes this to different role expectations: on the oncology ward nurses are expected to try to heal patients with cancer whereas in hospice programs the nurses' task is to accompany the terminally ill on their final journey. By defining the situation differently, perception and behavior of both patient and caregiver are altered.

The same applies at an institutional level. Recently a school on the West Coast had to close two of its buildings when seismographic standards were raised. To "retrofit" these beautiful structures with earthquake-resistant walls would cost between ten and fifteen million dollars, a sum well beyond the means of the institution. Unused, the two decaying buildings stand as symbols of a wealthy and powerful denominational past that is eroding all around the institution. One solution would be to *redefine the situation*. Rather than retain the old dream of a life-style of wealth and power, the school could turn a liability into an asset by converting the buildings into a museum of historic ruins of a bygone age, thus recognizing the vast changes that have taken place between religion and culture in contemporary America.

As mentioned earlier, the exilic prophets (Jeremiah, Second Isaiah, and Ezekiel) provide us with examples of how historical circumstances sometimes require a redefinition at the national level. Without their creative redefinition of God and God's work in history, the Jewish people as a religious entity might have ceased to exist.

In like manner, our nation also needs creative redefinition. The task of leadership is to assist our communities to embrace the night as a time of potential creativity, as a time when we are forced to focus and meditate on impasse. Darkness may feel like death when, in fact, new life is struggling to be born. Belden Lane notes that impasse "forces the right side of the brain into gear, seeking intuitive, symbolic, unconventional answers, so that action can be renewed eventually with greater purpose."[26]

Redefining the situation involves four major responsibilities: assisting people to name, to grieve, to relinquish, and to receive.[27] In *The Journey Is Home*, Nelle Morton describes the experience of women "hearing one another to speech."[28] We must listen like foreign-language tutors, helping each other to configure our mouths and our tongues and even to gesture with our bodies so that we can speak the language of loss, so that we can name the demons that haunt us. As long as we are silent, our feelings remain buried and inchoate. To name our dis-ease is to regain a modicum of power. To identify the characteristics of our plight allows us to walk around it, view it from all sides, make friends with it. This is not a ministry of counseling. It provides no answers and gives no advice. Instead, this ministry listens actively, passionately. This ministry seeks to "stand *under*" (*verstehen*) the frustration and the anger of impasse. It asks probing questions, clarifies meanings, explores experience.

Naming must unfold into grieving. Neither macho repression nor stoic acceptance will suffice. We must allow full play to the depth of our loss, alternating the wrenching sobs of abandonment with clenched-fisted cries of protest. "Real hope comes in, with and under grief," writes Brueggemann. "Only grief permits newness."[29] John of the Cross sees the grief experience as the necessary means for purging ourselves of the dark side of desire. Unlimited desires in a limited world devour us, leaving us restless, ever-grasping, longing, and climbing over others to appease insatiable appetites. As the vets will testify, without grief, there is no healing.

The third most popular theme in Christian art (after the Madonna and child and the crucifixion) is the *Pietà*, depicting Mary holding the pierced corpse of her son Jesus. Whether in sculpture or in painting, the focus is not so much on Jesus as on his grieving mother. Recently Eldon Olson, who is responsible for the pastoral care given by Lutheran (ELCA) clergy in the Northwest, described to me his work. "The best image I can come up with for ministry today," he said, "is that of the *Pietà*. We are undergoing a major transition in our history, and our people are suffering great losses. Now is the time to hold the corpse, to grieve and wait."

Grief prepares us to relinquish the old dream. Grief that only wails and blames is not enough. Grief must lead us to relinquish dreams that can no longer come true. In the mid-1970s, when North American theologians were struggling to come to terms with Latin American liberation theology and Third World demands for a new international economic order, Sr. Marie Augusta Neal wrote a book on the theology of relinquishment. When we discover how we rob the poor through the unjust structures of society, she said, we are less likely to resist when the poor reach out to take what is rightfully theirs.[30] Although the tone of Neal's book sounds somewhat dated now — the fabric of wealthy societies has come under such challenge that relinquishment takes on even vaster proportions today — her basic argument remains. The old dream of solving the distribution problem by equal opportunity, economic growth, and a modicum of welfare no longer works. We know now that community is fragile, requires careful nurture, and cannot be achieved by coercion (as communism tried) or left to the whims of market forces. But our impasse cannot be cured by these concessions. Now we are called upon to relinquish our accustomed place in the world, to reassess the meaning of our desire to be number one, to explore the evil imaginings that have fueled our Promethean hubris and brought us to the current impasse. The very sustaining capacity of the planet itself *requires* the demise of the American Dream. We are now challenged to relinquish that dream so that a new dream may rise from its ashes.

The dark night is an emptying experience. Naming, grieving, and relinquishing prepare us to receive. The new is not given on demand. It is beyond conscious, rational control. It cannot be managed by objectives. Instead, we must wait for it, persistently and patiently. In our waiting we can nourish hope amid the darkness not only by attending to the message of the exilic prophets, as Brueggemann suggests, but also by retelling the stories of modern prophets who have spoken and acted on the best in our nation's narrative.

Often a certain story may appear trivial or insignificant to an outsider, while expressing the full depth of mature hope for those who live within its narrative world. One such story is reenacted once a month in our local congregation and three times a day in the homes of many of our members. It started in 1976 with a simple suggestion by one woman in Florida. Recognizing the great suffering around the world from physical hunger, Rosellyn Calvert suggested that the members of her regional Presbyterian women's group contribute two cents a meal for twenty years — not to eliminate world hunger, but to increase their understanding and identification with the hungry. Since that time, the idea has spread across the country. I first heard about it in 1986 when our local church and our regional ecclesiastical body (the Presbytery of the Redwoods on the northern coast of California) decided to participate. At a designated time in the worship service on the last Sunday of every month, each family deposits its collected pennies in an offering basket at the foot of the Communion table.

Recently our interim minister instructed the congregation to deposit the pennies in a basket on the way out of the church. Many objected, leading us to recognize that over the years this simple act has taken on a depth of meaning that we are dimly aware of but unable to fully explain. Here is an issue — hunger — that defies human understanding. In the past forty years, agronomists, economists, political scientists, anthropologists, sociologists, philosophers, historians, and social ethicists from every ideological persuasion have harnessed their energies to study this problem and propose solutions. An enormous new industry has emerged, comprising United Nations agencies, regional intergovernmental agencies, private businesses, and nonprofit agencies, all dedicated to overcoming hunger and the other attendant elements of poverty. The cold war was fueled by competing solutions to the multiple problems of development that are symbolized by hunger. In spite of all the progress (technological, educational, attitudinal, and so on) made in certain countries, basic nutritional security for all people now appears as remote as ever before. As Latin American theologians have said, the war against the poor continues unabated. The whole world experiences impasse in this regard.

Rather than deny the impasse, Rosellyn Calvert chose to enter it, to name it, to grieve it, to relinquish any pretense of solving it, and to perform three times a day a symbolic act that puts her in solidarity with the hungry of the world. Our congregation resisted the interim minister's attempt to relegate this offering to an afterthought because we recognize a sacramental quality to this act. For us it has become a metaphorical act whereby we express our solidarity and communion with all who suffer from the absence of basic human needs. We know it is a small gesture; in fact some members collect their pennies in Band-Aid cans to remind themselves that handouts from the rich to the poor merely cover up the sores. But we also know that it is much more than a gesture. For us it has become a sacramental act expressing our active longing for the full reign of God when no person and no nation will live by narratives of exceptionalism that purchase self-esteem by denying it to others.

In recent years the military has developed special lenses for seeing in the dark. If ours is a time of "the dark night of the world," then we must develop our night vision. We must form communities of those who probe the darkness and go right to "the bottom of the night," so that even in such a time as ours they may "still persuade us to rejoice." Of such are new dreams born.

Notes

Preface

1. For an exploration of each of these themes, see Brian J. Walsh, *Langdon Gilkey: Theologian for a Culture in Decline* (Lanham, Md.: Univ. Press of America, 1991); James Davison Hunter, *Cultural Wars: The Struggle to Define America* (New York: Basic Books, 1991); and Walter Brueggemann, *Hopeful Imagination* (Philadelphia: Fortress, 1986).

2. John Carlos Rowe and Rick Berg, *The Vietnam War and American Culture* (New York: Columbia Univ. Press, 1991), 11.

Introduction

1. Stephen Schlosstein, *The End of the American Century* (Chicago: Congdon and Weed, 1989); David Calleo, *Beyond American Hegemony* (New York: Basic Books, 1987); Richard Rosecrance, *America's Economic Resurgence* (New York: Harper and Row, 1990); Henry R. Nau, *The Myth of America's Decline* (New York: Oxford Univ. Press, 1990). (Cited in Paul Kennedy, *Preparing for the Twenty-First Century* [New York: Random House, 1993], 290.)

2. Alice M. Rivlin, *Reviving the American Dream* (Washington, D.C.: Brookings Institution, 1993).

3. Kennedy, *Preparing for the Twenty-First Century*, 324.

4. Richard Holbrooke, in *The Bad War: An Oral History of the Vietnam War*, ed. Kim Willenson (New York: NAL, 1987), 398.

5. Ron Hudspeth, *Atlanta Constitution*, April 26, 1980.

6. Robert Divine has shown that following American wars, historical interpretation usually goes through three stages: (1) a repudiation of the policies that led to war; (2) a revisionist support for those policies; and (3) a synthesis of stages 1 and 2 ("Historiography: Vietnam Reconsidered," *Diplomatic History* 12 [Winter 1988]: 79–93). Influential revisionist interpretations include the following: Guenter Lewy, *America in Vietnam* (New York: Oxford Univ. Press, 1978); Norman Podhoretz, *Why We Were in Vietnam* (New York: Simon and Schuster, 1982); Harry G. Summers, Jr., *On Strategy: A Critical Analysis of the Viet-*

nam War (Novato, Calif.: Presidio, 1982); and Richard Nixon, *No More Vietnams* (New York: Avon, 1986). Summers's book is particularly important because he is a professor at the Army War College and his book is being used as a text there, at the Army Command and General Staff College, at the Marine Corps Amphibious Warfare School, at the National Defense University, and at the Air and Naval War Colleges. His book was determinative in shaping U.S. military policy during the Gulf War. His most recent book, *On Strategy II: A Critical Analysis of the Gulf War* (New York: Dell, 1992), pursues an argument similar to the one he made in his earlier book on Vietnam.

7. Charles Krauthammer, "How the War Can Change America," *Time Magazine*, January 28, 1991, 100.

8. "Fragging" refers to killing a fellow soldier or officer, usually with a fragmentation grenade. The incidence of fraggings among U.S. troops increased in the latter years of the war when large numbers of draftees had become thoroughly disillusioned.

9. Peter Applebome, "At Home, War Healed Several Wounds," *New York Times*, February 26, 1991, p. A1.

10. Gary Wills, *Under God: Religion and American Politics* (New York: Simon and Schuster, 1990), 25.

11. James Davison Hunter, *Culture Wars: The Struggle to Define America* (New York: Basic Books, 1991), 50.

12. Robert Stone, *Dog Soldiers* (Boston: Houghton Mifflin, 1973), 56–57.

13. See Walter Brueggemann, *The Prophetic Imagination* (Philadelphia: Fortress, 1978), for a discussion of these two forms of consciousness within the biblical story.

14. See chapter 5 for a fuller discussion of American Exceptionalism.

15. During the period of Reconstruction monuments to the Confederate soldiers were erected in town squares all across the South. Many of these give testimony still today to that effort to deny and repress the demons that gave rise to the war. In my father's hometown, Lancaster, South Carolina, the inscription on the monument reads: "GOD HOLDS THE SCALES OF JUSTICE. HE WILL MEASURE PRAISE AND BLAME. AND THE SOUTH WILL STAND THE VERDICT AND WILL STAND IT WITHOUT SHAME." The monument in Tuscombia, Alabama, near my childhood home, reads: "THE MEN WERE RIGHT WHO WORE THE GREY AND TRUTH CAN NEVER DIE. THE MANNER OF THEIR DEATH WAS THE CROWNING GLORY OF THEIR LIVES."

16. A number of chaplains who served in Vietnam have written journal articles and personal memoirs. Only two books have been published, to my knowledge, examining the war experience from an explicitly theological frame of reference. These are William P. Mahedy's

Out of the Night (New York: Ballantine, 1986), and Uwe Siemon-Netto's *The Acquittal of God* (New York: Pilgrim, 1990).

17. James Webb, cited in Timothy Lomperis, *Reading the Wind: The Literature of the Vietnam War* (Durham, N.C.: Duke Univ. Press, 1987), 44. Lomperis goes on to explain this great diversity: "In fleshing out just how varied this experience of Vietnam was, John Del Vecchio tried to present a three-dimensional graphic representation of this diversity. On the x-axis he drew the time line of John Clark Pratt's seven-act play (including the prologue and epilogue) of the Vietnam War. On the y-axis he put down the seven topographical regions in which the Indochina war was fought. On these two axes alone, you get a grid of forty-nine possibilities. Adding a z-axis to incorporate a minimum of personal characteristics like age, rank, race, education, and military job, you can get as many as five hundred different experiences. No wonder the literature still lacks a unifying theme and remains fragmented" (pp. 44–45).

18. James Bond Stockdale and Sybil B. Stockdale, *In Love and War* (New York: Harper and Row, 1984).

19. Henri Nouwen, *The Wounded Healer* (New York: Image, 1979), 72.

20. Personal interview with John Fergueson. See also his article "A Man of Sorrows, Familiar with Suffering," *The Olympia Churchman* (July/August, 1985): 6.

Chapter One: Identity

1. *San Francisco Sunday Examiner and Chronicle*, July 19, 1992, p. 3, Sunday Punch section.

2. Lynn Ludlow, "Doors Foreclosing on American Dream," *San Francisco Sunday Examiner and Chronicle*, August 2, 1992, p. 1.

3. George W. Stroup, *The Promise of Narrative Theology* (Atlanta: John Knox, 1981), 132–33.

4. John Hellmann, *American Myth and the Legacy of Vietnam* (New York: Columbia Univ. Press, 1986).

5. See Hans Mol, *Identity and the Sacred: A Sketch for a New Social-Scientific Theory of Religion* (Oxford: Basil Blackwell, 1976), for a theologically informed sociological treatment of these four elements as they apply to the processes of identity formation, maintenance, reinforcement, and alteration.

6. Ibid., 59.

7. In their most recent work, *The Good Society* (New York: Alfred A. Knopf, 1991), Robert Bellah and colleagues show how every sector of U.S. society, including schools, religious bodies, and even family life, is dominated by market expectations and the economic roles we play.

Any leader of a declining congregation is aware of the effect of these subtle forces on even the most basic decisions.

8. Gary S. Gregg's recent work, *Self-Representation: Life Narrative Studies in Identity and Ideology* (New York: Greenwood, 1991), provides a fine critique of contemporary identity theory. Building on the more classical works of William James, George Herbert Mead, and Erik H. Erikson, Gregg proposes a solution to the unity-in-diversity problem by regarding identity (he calls it "self-representation") as a semiotic system consisting of three levels: the indexical, the metaphorical, and the ontological.

9. Erik H. Erikson, "The Problem of Ego Identity," in *Identity and Anxiety*, ed. Maurice R. Stein, Arthur J. Vidich, and David Manning White (Glencoe, Ill.: Free Press, 1960), 30 (cited by Mol, *Identity and the Sacred*, 57).

10. H. Richard Niebuhr, *The Meaning of Revelation* (New York: Macmillan, 1960), 80.

11. Hans Mol, ed., *Identity and Religion: International, Cross-Cultural Approaches* (Beverly Hills, Calif.: Sage, 1978), 10. If each of us were to draw our own diagram, it might have a fourth level representing a commitment to a yet-to-be-formed social reality that transcends the nation-state, and also a fifth level representing a transcendental dimension like the kingdom of God. Likewise, at the second level we would have a cluster of groups including family, work, and a variety of voluntary associations, each reinforcing the others but at the same time in tension with the others.

12. Robert A. Krieg, *Story-Shaped Christology* (Mahwah, N.J.: Paulist, 1988), 9ff.

13. Cited by John Shea, *Stories of God* (Chicago: Thomas More, 1978), 41–42.

14. Viktor Frankl, *Man's Search for Meaning* (New York: Washington Square, 1963), 154.

15. A. J. Ungersma, *The Search for Meaning* (Philadelphia: Westminster, 1961), 26–27.

16. Robert Mason, *Chickenhawk* (New York: Penguin, 1984).

17. Peter Berger, *The Social Reality of Religion* (London: Penguin, 1973), 28–30.

18. Stephen Crites, "The Narrative Quality of Experience," *Journal of the American Academy of Religion* 39, no. 3 (September 1971): 291–311.

19. Barbara Hardy, "Towards a Poetics of Fiction: An Approach through Narrative," *Novel* 2 (1968): 5 (cited by Alasdair MacIntyre, *After Virtue* [Notre Dame, Ind.: Univ. of Notre Dame Press, 1981], 211).

20. A volume edited by Stanley Hauerwas and L. Gregory Jones, *Why Narrative? Readings in Narrative Theology* (Grand Rapids: Eerd-

mans, 1989), provides the best current overview of the nature and functions of narrative.

21. Terrence W. Tilley, *Story Theology* (Collegeville, Minn.: Michael Glazier, 1985), 35.

22. John Dominic Crossan, *The Dark Interval* (Allen, Tex.: Argus, 1975), 9.

23. See John C. Hoffman, *Law, Freedom, and Story* (Waterloo, Ont.: Wilfrid Laurier Univ. Press, 1986), 33ff.

24. Orrin E. Klapp, *Collective Search for Identity* (New York: Holt, Rinehart and Winston, 1969).

25. Mol, *Identity and the Sacred*, 216.

26. Ibid., 5–8.

27. Tom F. Driver, *The Magic of Ritual* (San Francisco: Harper, 1991), 147; emphasis added.

28. I am indebted to the following for my interpretation of Van Gennep and Turner: Hoffman, *Law, Freedom, and Story*; Kali Tal, "Speaking the Language of Pain: Vietnam War Literature in the Context of a Literature of Trauma," in *Fourteen Landing Zones*, ed. Philip K. Jason (Iowa City: Univ. of Iowa Press, 1991), 217–50; and Driver, *Magic of Ritual*.

29. Arnold Van Gennep, *Rites of Passage*, trans. Monika B Vizedom and Gabrielle L. Caffee (Chicago: Univ. of Chicago Press, 1960).

30. Driver, *Magic of Ritual*, 157.

31. Victor Turner, *The Ritual Process* (New York: Penguin, 1969), 81 (cited by Driver, *Magic of Ritual*, 158).

32. Driver, *Magic of Ritual*, 131–91.

33. Crossan, *Dark Interval*, 9. Turner uses the terms "structure," "anti-structure," and "counter-structure" to point to similar processes at work in rituals.

34. Driver, *Magic of Ritual*, 135.

35. Robert Grimes, *Symbol and Conquest* (Ithaca, N.Y.: Cornell Univ. Press, 1976).

36. Ibid., 163 (cited by Hoffman, *Law, Freedom, and Story*, 77).

37. Driver, *Magic of Ritual*, 137.

38. Al Hubbard, executive secretary of the Vietnam Veterans Against the War, as cited by Marilyn B. Young, *The Vietnam Wars, 1945–1990* (New York: HarperCollins, 1991), 256.

39. Driver, *Magic of Ritual*, 159.

40. Turner, *Ritual Process*, 82 (cited by Driver, *Magic of Ritual*, 160).

41. Ibid. (cited by Driver, *Magic of Ritual*, 161).

42. Victor Turner, *Dramas, Fields, and Metaphors: Symbolic Action in Human Society* (Ithaca, N.Y.: Cornell Univ. Press, 1974), 47.

43. Driver, *Magic of Ritual*, 181.

44. Western science has not found adequate ways to describe or explain the power that resides in rituals. Magic is the name given this

power by theologians and anthropologists alike. Driver recognizes the necessity of dealing with this issue head on. His summary of the anthropological debate over magic, science, and religion is the best I have come across. He concludes that both religious and "secular" rituals do involve magic, but not in the fantastical sense. "The word 'magic,' which serves to remind us that ritual is a means of confronting power with power, is also a reminder that not all power is physical and material" (Driver, *Magic of Ritual*, 172).

45. Victor Turner, *The Anthropology of Performance* (New York: Performing Arts Journal Publications, 1986), 24 (cited by Driver, *Magic of Ritual*, 189).

Chapter Two:
The Generic Vietnam War Narrative

1. Rudolf Otto writes: "These two qualities, the daunting and the fascinating, now combine in a strange harmony of contrasts....The daemonic-divine object may appear to the mind an object of horror and dread, but at the same time it is no less something that allures with a potent charm....The 'mystery' is for him not merely something to be wondered at but something that entrances him; and beside that in it which bewilders and confounds, he feels a something that captivates and transports him with a strange ravishment, rising often to the pitch of dizzy intoxication; it is the Dionysiac-element in the numen" (*The Idea of the Holy*, trans. John W. Harvey [1958; reprint, New York: Oxford Univ. Press, 1970], 31).

2. Kali Tal labels Vietnam War writings a "literature of trauma" that gives voice to the survivors' compulsion to bear witness ("Speaking the Language of Pain: Vietnam War Literature in the Context of a Literature of Trauma," in *Fourteen Landing Zones*, ed. Philip K. Jason [Iowa City: Univ. of Iowa Press, 1991], 217–50).

3. Timothy J. Lomperis and John Clark Pratt, *Reading the Wind: The Literature of the Vietnam War* (Durham, N.C.: Duke Univ. Press, 1987), 113.

4. John Newman, librarian of the special collection of Vietnam fiction at Colorado State University, reports that even now, twenty years after the war, vets are still churning out an average of thirty new novels per year.

5. Each of these perspectives finds voice not only in oral and written narrative but also in film and scholarly writing.

6. Lomperis and Pratt, *Reading the Wind*, 124–25. In *Vietnam Voices* (New York: Penguin, 1984), John Clark Pratt uses this pattern to organize his historical documentation of the war. He maintains that given the complexity of the wars in Indochina, all we can do is form a

"collage" of the fragments that, when put together, most resemble a Shakespearean tragedy.

7. See the articles in Owen W. Gilman, Jr., and Lorrie Smith, eds., *America Rediscovered* (New York: Garland, 1990).

8. Philip Beidler, *American Literature and the Experience of Vietnam* (Athens: Univ. of Georgia Press, 1982), 113.

9. Timothy O'Brien, *Going after Cacciato* (New York: Dell, 1978).

10. Stephen Wright, *Meditations in Green* (New York: Bantam, 1984).

11. C. D. B. Bryan, "Barely Suppressed Screams," *Harpers*, June 1984, 67–72.

12. An FNG (fucking new guy) was a replacement for a buddy killed or wounded in action. Because replacements were untested in battle and as yet uninitiated into the ways of the Brotherhood, they were treated with caution and resentment until they proved themselves. The term FNG connotes the complex emotional responses of seasoned soldiers toward the war, their losses, and the vulnerability of once again trusting their lives to novices.

13. Jack Fuller, *Fragments* (New York: Dell, 1984), 79.

14. Bryan, "Barely Suppressed Screams," 69.

15. The alternation among these three styles is baffling at times, as if three different languages are being spoken. This is one of the characteristics that distinguishes the Vietnam War narratives from those of earlier wars. It is so prevalent that one wonders why so little attention has been given to this phenomenon. This discussion draws upon one of the very few technical analyses, the excellent article by J. T. Hansen, "Vocabularies of Experience," in Gilman and Smith, *America Rediscovered*, 134–49.

16. J. T. Hansen describes how the single word "motherfucker," often pronounced "muh-thuh-fuck-uh," takes on all these connotations, depending upon the context and the circumstance ("Vocabularies of Experience," 141–44).

17. Michael Herr, *Dispatches* (1968; reprint, New York: Avon, 1978), 92–93.

18. T. S. Eliot, *Selected Essays* (New York: Harcourt, Brace and Co., 1950), 248 (cited by Hansen, "Vocabularies of Experience," 141).

19. For a discussion of fragging, see the introduction, n. 8, above.

20. Former army chief of chaplains General Kermit Johnson notes that George Washington's order barring profanity is still observed by most officers, but that this "purity" is purchased at the expense of enlisted men who do the dirty work (private correspondence, June 19, 1993; see also Kermit Johnson, "Ethical Issues in Military Leadership," *Parameters* 4, no. 2 [1974]: 35–39).

21. Philip Caputo, *A Rumor of War* (New York: Ballantine, 1977), 157–58.

22. Soldiers are honor-bound to remove the wounded and the dead from the field of battle even at great risk to themselves. The fierce anger of veterans and their families toward the U.S. government for abandoning POWs and MIAs in Indochina after the war and then lying about it derives from this sense of betrayal by the chain of command.

23. Kennedy was merely giving vigorous new expression to a previous officially sanctioned mythos. A full-blown rationale for understanding the cold war in Manichaean terms found expression in a study commissioned by President Truman in 1950 called NSC-68. Authored by Paul Nitze and Dean Acheson, this secret document, which was not declassified until 1975, became the blueprint for a policy of containment. It idealized the United States and demonized the Soviet Union, and in so doing prepared the ground for the moral corruption that the U.S. military inflicted upon itself in Vietnam. Because of the enormity of the Soviet evil, any means was deemed justified to repel this threat: "The integrity of our system will not be jeopardized by any measures, covert or overt, violent or non-violent, which serve the purpose of frustrating the Kremlin design, nor does the necessity for conducting ourselves so as to affirm our values in actions as well as words forbid such measures, provided only they are appropriately calculated to that end and are not so excessive or misdirected as to make us enemies of the people instead of the evil men who have enslaved them" (NSC-68, April 14, 1950, FR:1950, I, 243–44). Later Acheson admitted that the polemical tone of this cold war blueprint was intentional: "The purpose of NSC-68 was to so bludgeon the mass mind of 'top government' that not only could the President make a decision but that the decision could be carried out" (Dean Acheson, *Present at the Creation: My Years in the State Department* [New York: Norton, 1969], 374 [cited in John Lewis Gaddis, *Strategies of Containment* (New York: Oxford Univ. Press, 1982), 99–100]).

24. William Lederer and Eugene Burdick, *The Ugly American* (New York: Norton, 1958). See John Hellmann, *American Myth and the Legacy of Vietnam* (New York: Columbia Univ. Press, 1986), 3–35, for the fascinating story of the influence of this book on the Kennedy presidency.

25. Caputo, *A Rumor of War*, xiv.

26. Herr, *Dispatches*, 64.

27. Robert Mason, *Chickenhawk* (New York: Penguin, 1984), 473.

28. Ibid., 467–68.

29. Tal, "Speaking the Language of Pain," 226–27. Tal relates the literature on trauma to the experiences of survivors of the American Civil War, World War I, World War II, the Holocaust, and incest and other forms of domestic violence.

30. Elie Wiesel, "Why I Write," in *Confronting the Holocaust: The Impact of Elie Wiesel*, ed. Alvin H. Rosenfeld and Irving Greenberg

(Bloomington: Indiana Univ. Press, 1978), 200–201 (cited by Tal, "Speaking the Language of Pain," 229–30).

31. Fuller, *Fragments*, 210.

32. Ibid.

33. Caputo, *A Rumor of War*, xiii.

34. See Lomperis and Pratt, *Reading the Wind*, 105–6.

35. David Halberstam, correspondent for the *New York Times*, published his first book on Vietnam, *The Making of a Quagmire* (New York: Alfred A. Knopf), in 1965.

Chapter Three: The Heart of Darkness

1. No single person who served in Vietnam embodied the classic spirit of American military heroism more fully than Lieutenant Colonel John Paul Vann. His career is brilliantly portrayed in Neil Sheehan's historical biography, *A Bright Shining Lie* (New York: Vintage, 1988), which won the National Book Award and the Pulitzer Prize for Nonfiction. Vann's story is a tragic parable of the American journey in Vietnam.

2. See Richard Slotkin, *Regeneration through Violence: The Mythology of the American Frontier, 1600–1860* (Middletown, Conn.: Wesleyan Univ. Press, 1973).

3. Quoted by Roger I. Shinn, *Wars and Rumors of Wars* (Nashville: Abingdon, 1972), 261–62.

4. Jack Fuller, *Fragments* (New York: Dell, 1984), 57.

5. This cartoon appeared in a GI underground newspaper, *Gigline*, published at Fort Bliss, Texas, in the early 1970s. Skip Delano furnished a photograph of it for inclusion in this text.

6. Francis Coppola's film *Apocalypse Now* is based upon Conrad's novella. Several writers also make use of Conrad's framework to explore the American experience in Vietnam. See Tobey C. Herzog, "John Wayne in a Modern Heart of Darkness: The American Soldier in Vietnam," in *Search and Clear: Critical Responses to Selected Literature and Films of the Vietnam War*, ed. William J. Searle (Bowling Green, Ohio: Bowling Green State Univ. Popular Press, 1988), 16–29; Catherine Calloway, "The Vietnam Novel: A Descent into Hell" (Ph.D. Diss., University of South Florida, 1987); J. Terry Frazier, "Vietnam War Stories Looking at the Heart of Darkness," *Studies in Popular Culture* 5 (1982): 1–6; Galen Meyer, "The Vietnam War and Joseph Conrad's Heart of Darkness," *Pro Rege* 11, no. 4 (1983): 2–12. Only recently have the critics discovered in John Clark Pratt's 1974 novel, *Laotian Fragments* (New York: Viking), that the interpretive framework for the wars in Southeast Asia is that of Joseph Conrad's *Heart of Darkness*. See James

Aubrey, "Conradian 'Darkness' in John Pratt's *Laotian Fragments*," *Conradiana* 2, no. 2 (1990): 83–93. The text of Conrad's novella used in the present work is that included in *Heart of Darkness: A Case Study in Contemporary Criticism*, ed. Ross C. Murfin (New York: St. Martin's, 1989). All direct citations from Conrad are from this version of the text.

7. Herzog, "John Wayne," 18–21.

8. Ibid., 16.

9. Conrad, *Heart of Darkness*, 26.

10. Octave Mannoni, *Prospero and Caliban: The Psychology of Colonization* (New York: Praeger, 1964).

11. William Broyles, Jr., "Why Men Love War," *Esquire*, November 1984, 61.

12. Philip Caputo, *A Rumor of War* (New York: Ballantine, 1977). All citations in the text refer to this edition of the work.

13. W. Taylor Stevenson, "The Experience of Defilement: A Response to John Wheeler," *Anglican Theological Review* 64 (January 1982): 15–29.

14. During the Gulf War, I interviewed a number of Vietnam vets who were protesting that war. One carried a sign that read "Support Our Boys. Bring 'Em Home!" None of those I interviewed who were strongly opposed to the war thought it was possible to "support" (affirm and encourage) the troops without supporting the war itself. They also agreed that opposition to the war would undermine troop morale.

Chapter Four: Abjection

1. Helen Merrell Lynd, *On Shame and the Search for Identity* (New York: Harcourt, Brace and Co., 1958), chap. 2.

2. William Turner Huggett, *Body Count* (New York: Dell, 1973).

3. William P. Mahedy, *Out of the Night* (New York: Ballantine, 1986), 4.

4. Lynd, *On Shame*, 56–57.

5. See Julia Kristeva, *Powers of Horror: An Essay on Abjection*, trans. Leon S. Roudiez (New York: Columbia Univ. Press, 1982).

6. Kristeva, *Powers of Horror*, 4.

7. William Broyles, Jr., "Why Men Love War," *Esquire*, November 1984, 57–58.

8. Kristeva, *Powers of Horror*, 9.

9. Ibid., 4.

10. Ibid., 205–6.

11. Jack Fuller, *Fragments* (New York: Dell, 1984), 84–86.

12. Kristeva, *Powers of Horror*, 1.

13. Philip Caputo, *A Rumor of War* (New York: Ballantine, 1977), 254.

14. Kristeva, *Powers of Horror*, 5.

15. Leon S. Roudiez, who translated Kristeva's *Powers of Horror* into English, directs the reader's attention to her Freudian assumption regarding the relationship between meaninglessness and loss. "The object *a* is mentioned twice, and it could be puzzling. A few lines from Stuart Schneiderman's *Returning to Freud* (Yale Univ. Press, 1980) might prove helpful: 'For the psychoanalyst the important object is the lost object, the object always desired and never attained, the object that causes the subject to desire in cases where he can never gain the satisfaction of possessing the object. Any object the subject desires will never be anything other than a substitute for the object *a*" (translator's note, x). This is a latter-day echo of a statement made by a much earlier psychologist, Augustine of Hippo, when he recognized that nothing in this life brings lasting satisfaction: "Thou hast made us for thyself, O God, and our hearts are restless until they find their rest in Thee."

16. Philip Beidler, *American Literature and the Experience of Vietnam* (Athens: Univ. of Georgia Press, 1982), 162.

17. Gustav Hasford, *The Short-Timers* (New York: Harper and Row, 1979). Page references in the text are to this edition of the work. Hasford's novel, it should be noted, is the basis for Stanley Kubrick's film on the Vietnam War, *Full Metal Jacket*.

18. Thomas Myers, *Walking Point: American Narratives of Vietnam* (New York: Oxford Univ. Press, 1988), 212.

19. Terry Frazier, "Vietnam War Stories Looking at the Heart of Darkness," *Studies in Popular Culture* 5 (1982): 4.

20. Robert Stone, *Dog Soldiers* (Boston: Houghton Mifflin, 1973), 56–57.

21. John Hellmann, *American Myth and the Legacy of Vietnam* (New York: Columbia Univ. Press, 1986), 188–202. My "take" on the film is generally in line with Hellmann's, but I have also found helpful interpretations in Albert Auster and Leonard Quart, *How the War Was Remembered: Hollywood and Vietnam* (New York: Praeger, 1988).

22. Hellmann, *American Myth*, 199.

Chapter Five:
Coming Home to a God that Failed

1. Robert Bly, "The Erosion of Male Confidence," in *Vietnam in Remission*, ed. James F. Veninga and Harry A. Wilmer (College Station: Texas A & M Univ. Press, 1985), 58–75.

2. Unpublished typescript entitled "Impact of War from the Perspective of a Vietnam Combat Veteran." An address given in the late 1980s at the Water Tower in Louisville, Kentucky, during an event sponsored by WHAS Radio and TV.

3. Paul Fussell, "The Real War 1939–1945," *The Atlantic Monthly,* August 1989, 34.

4. H. Richard Niebuhr, *The Meaning of Revelation* (New York: Macmillan, 1960), 99ff.

5. William J. Searle, "Walking Wounded: Vietnam War Novels of Return," in *Search and Clear: Critical Responses to Selected Literature and Films of the Vietnam War,* ed. William J. Searle (Bowling Green, Ohio: Bowling Green State Univ. Popular Press, 1988), 151.

6. Peter Marin, "Living in Moral Pain," *Psychology Today,* November 1981, 74.

7. Cited by Fussell, "The Real War," 36.

8. J. T. Hansen, A. Susan Owen, and Michael Patrick Madden, *Parallels: The Soldiers' Knowledge and the Oral History of Contemporary Warfare* (New York: Aldine de Gruyter, 1992), 123.

9. Charles Coleman, *Sergeant Back Again* (New York: Harper and Row, 1980), 119.

10. George W. Stroup, *The Promise of Narrative Theology* (Atlanta: John Knox, 1981), 171ff.

11. Timothy O'Brien, *Going after Cacciato* (New York: Dell, 1978), 320–21.

12. John Hellmann, *American Myth and the Legacy of Vietnam* (New York: Columbia Univ. Press, 1986), x.

13. Loren Baritz, *Backfire: A History of How American Culture Led Us into Vietnam and Made Us Fight the Way We Did* (New York: William Morrow, 1985).

14. See R. W. B. Lewis, *The New American Adam* (Chicago: Univ. of Chicago Press, 1955).

15. See Ernest Lee Tuveson, *Redeemer Nation: The Idea of America's Millennial Role* (Chicago: Univ. of Chicago Press, 1968).

16. See Leo Marx, *The Machine in the Garden: Technology and the Pastoral Ideal in America* (New York: Oxford Univ. Press, 1964).

17. Quoted by Loren Baritz, *Backfire,* 316.

18. Ibid., 324.

19. Robert Jewett, *The Captain America Complex* (Philadelphia: Westminster, 1973).

20. Quoted by Baritz, *Backfire,* 324, 328.

21. See Sydney Mead, *The Nation with the Soul of a Church* (New York: Harper and Row, 1975).

22. See Walter Holbling, "Literary Sense-Making: Vietnam Fiction," in *Vietnam Images: War and Representation,* ed. Jeffrey Walsh and James Aulich (New York: St Martin's, 1989), 134.

23. The book was first published by Harper in 1949.

24. Mahedy and others discuss this in terms of the idolatry of American civil religion. I prefer to use the more emotive, nationalistic

term "Americanism," which captures a dimension of personal devotion that has been neglected in the debates about American civil religion.

25. Peter Marin, "Living in Moral Pain," *Psychology Today,* November 1981, 68–80.

26. Emil Brunner, *Faith, Hope and Love* (Philadelphia: Westminster, 1956) 13. Although Brunner does, not acknowledge any indebtedness to Augustine, the fourth-century theologian pointed in the same direction in his *Confessions.* See Stephen Crites, "The Narrative Quality of Experience," in *Why Narrative? Readings in Narrative Theology,* ed. Stanley Hauerwas and L. Gregory Jones (Grand Rapids: Eerdmans, 1989), 72–84.

27. Crites, "Narrative Quality," 77.

28. Ron Kovic in Timothy J. Lomperis and John Clark Pratt, *Reading the Wind: The Literature of the Vietnam War* (Durham, N.C.: Duke Univ. Press, 1987), 34.

29. This pattern is amply documented by the *Pentagon Papers,* which Daniel Ellsberg leaked to the *New York Times* in the spring of 1971.

30. The other two plays are *The Basic Training of Pavlo Hummel* and *Streamers.* In this chapter the version of *Sticks and Bones* cited is from John Gasner, ed., *Best American Plays, 1967–1973* (New York: Crown, 1975), 245–82.

Chapter Six: The Dark Night

1. Jeremiah reports God's contention against prophet and priest: "They have healed the wound of my people lightly, saying 'Peace, peace,' when there is no peace" (Jeremiah 6:14; RSV).

2. Personal interview, March 15, 1991. Walter Capps teaches in the religious studies department of the University of California at Santa Barbara. Since 1979, he has taught an annual course on the American war in Vietnam, each time with an enrollment of over nine hundred students, many of whom are vets.

3. Robert Jay Lifton, *Home from the War* (Boston: Beacon, 1992), 121.

4. Robert Lifton's conclusion ("Guilt becomes the fulcrum on which the psychological destiny of the Vietnam survivor turns" [*Home from the War,* 108]) may apply to those he studied, all of whom joined the antiwar movement. But recent studies of shame imply that Lifton's generalization may not apply to all veterans. See Donald Capps, *The Depleted Self* (Philadelphia: Fortress, 1993); Michael Lewis, *Shame: The Exposed Self* (New York: Free Press, 1992); Donald L. Nathanson, ed., *The Many Faces of Shame* (New York: Guilford, 1987).

5. George C. Wilson, "Back to the Land of the Nightmares," *San Francisco Sunday Examiner and Chronicle,* March 18, 1990, p. 8, Sunday Punch section.

6. M. J. Horowitz, *Stress Response Syndromes* (New York: Jason Aronson, 1976).

7. William P. Mahedy, *Out of the Night* (New York: Ballantine, 1984), 78.

8. Personal interview with Walter Capps, March 15, 1991.

9. Peter Marin, "Living in Moral Pain," *Psychology Today*, November 1981, 68–80.

10. Lifton made this same point in the early 1970s even before the term "post–traumatic stress disorder" was coined (*Home from the War*, 447–48).

11. Harry G. Summers, Jr., *On Strategy: A Critical Analysis of the Vietnam War* (Novato, Calif.: Presidio, 1982). Summer's book about the Gulf War, *On Strategy II* (New York: Dell, 1992), also divorces war from the larger framework of morality and meaning.

12. Martha Nussbaum, "Narrative Emotions: Beckett's Genealogy of Love," in *Why Narrative? Readings in Narrative Theology*, ed. Stanley Hauerwas and L. Gregory Jones (Grand Rapids: Eerdmans, 1989), 217.

13. Ibid., 218.

14. Ibid., 218, 224.

15. Arthur Egendorf, *Healing from the War* (Boston: Houghton Mifflin, 1985), 163ff.

16. Constance FitzGerald, O.C.D., "Impasse and Dark Night," in *Women's Spirituality*, ed. Joann Wolski Conn (New York: Paulist, 1986), 288.

17. Bobbie Ann Mason, *In Country* (New York: Harper and Row, 1985), 225.

18. FitzGerald, "Impasse and Dark Night," 288.

19. Dorothee Soelle, *Suffering* (Philadelphia: Fortress, 1975), 85 (cited by FitzGerald, "Impasse and Dark Night," 298).

20. Mary Caygill, "A Theology and Practice of Hope: A Ministry in the Context of Ecclesial and Societal 'Death'" (Doctor of Ministry Dissertation Project, San Francisco Theological Seminary, 1993), 5.

21. FitzGerald, "Impasse and Dark Night," 290–91.

22. Roger G. Betsworth, *Social Ethics* (Louisville: Westminster/John Knox, 1990), chap. 1.

23. H. Richard Niebuhr, *The Meaning of Revelation* (New York: Macmillan, 1960), 109.

24. Egendorf, *Healing*, 158.

25. Retired General Kermit Johnson has reminded me that the military chaplaincy is but an extension of the overall alliance between church and state in the United States whereby the state grants tax-exemption to the churches in exchange for religious legitimization of the state (personal correspondence, June 19, 1993). I recognize the need

for chaplains in the military, but I favor a restructuring of the relationship. As long as chaplains are officers in the military, role conflicts are inevitable, giving rise to perceptions like those that the grunts had of chaplains in Vietnam.

26. Mahedy, *Out of the Night,* 112.
27. Lifton, *Home from the War,* 167.
28. Ibid.
29. William Broyles, Jr., "Why Men Love War," *Esquire,* November 1984, 58.
30. Ibid., 62.
31. Niebuhr, *Meaning of Revelation,* 110.
32. Egendorf, *Healing from the War,* 132.

Chapter Seven: Hope in a Time of Impasse

1. Personal conversation with Roy Fairchild.
2. Richard Slotkin, *Gunfighter Nation* (New York: Atheneum, 1992), 59.
3. Figure 7 is taken from Gerald A. Arbuckle, S.M., "Organizations Must Ritually Grieve," *Human Development* 12, no. 1 (Spring 1991): 25.
4. Richard John Neuhaus, *The Naked Public Square* (Grand Rapids: Eerdmans, 1984), 154, vii, 102, 191, 60.
5. Don Buteyn, currently pastor of the First Presbyterian Church in Bakersfield, California, recounted his experience of being invited to the White House in the mid-1980s for a briefing on American policy toward Central America. At the time he was dean of San Francisco Theological Seminary, with strong connections in both liberal and conservative religious circles. When the group of religious leaders had heard the government briefing on political policy, they were taken to the offices of the IRD, whose leaders briefed them on religious dimensions of the Central American conflicts as interpreted by the religious right. Whence Buteyn's reference to the IRD as the Department of Religion of the Reagan presidency.
6. "Christianity and Democracy: A Statement of the Institute on Religion and Democracy" (Washington, D.C., 1981), 9.
7. George M. Marsden, "Are Secularists the Threat? Is Religion the Solution?" in *Unsecular America,* ed. Richard J. Neuhaus (Grand Rapids: Eerdmans, 1986), 49.
8. Stanley Hauerwas and William Willimon, *Resident Aliens* (Nashville: Abingdon, 1989), 32–33.
9. Ibid., 83.
10. Ibid., 47.
11. Ibid., 159.

12. For this summary of Brueggemann's position I have drawn upon four of his writings: "The Costly Loss of Lament," *Journal for the Study of the Old Testament*, no. 36 (1986): 57–71; *Hopeful Imagination* (Philadelphia: Fortress, 1986); "Disciplines of Readiness," Occasional Paper No. 1, Theology and Worship Unit, Presbyterian Church (U.S.A.) (Louisville, 1989); and "Preaching to Exiles," *Journal for Preachers* 16, no. 4 (Pentecost, 1993): 3–15. The last article contains references to recent scholarship on the exilic and postexilic periods.

13. Robert Bellah et al., *Habits of the Heart* (Berkeley: Univ. of California Press, 1985), and idem, *The Good Society* (New York: Alfred A. Knopf, 1991).

14. William M. Sullivan, *Reconstructing Public Philosophy* (Berkeley: Univ. of California Press, 1986).

15. Ibid., 12.

16. Ibid., xii.

17. Fred Hirsch, *Social Limits to Growth* (Cambridge, Mass.: Harvard Univ. Press, 1976); Daniel Bell, *The Cultural Contradictions of Capitalism* (New York: Basic Books, 1978); and Robert Heilbroner, *Business Civilization in Decline* (New York: Norton, 1976).

18. Sullivan, *Reconstructing Public Philosophy*, 28.

19. Bellah et al., *The Good Society*, 90ff.

20. Ronald Thiemann, *Constructing a Public Theology: The Church in a Pluralistic Culture* (Louisville: Westminster/John Knox, 1991), 90, 119.

21. Sullivan, *Reconstructing Public Philosophy*, xiii.

22. Thiemann, *Constructing a Public Theology*, chaps. 1, 4, and 6.

23. Constance FitzGerald, O.C.D., "Impasse and Dark Night," in *Women's Spirituality*, ed. Joann Wolski Conn (New York: Paulist, 1986), 288.

24. Ibid., 294.

25. Douglas John Hall, *Lighten Our Darkness* (Philadelphia: Westminster, 1976), chap. 1.

26. Belden Lane, "Spirituality and Political Commitment: Notes on a Liberation Theology of Nonviolence," *America*, March 14, 1981 (cited by FitzGerald, "Impasse and Dark Night," 289).

27. See the four works of Brueggemann listed above for extensive treatment of the way in which the prophets of the exile assisted Judah in these tasks.

28. Nelle Morton, *The Journey Is Home* (Boston: Beacon, 1985), 82.

29. Brueggemann, *Hopeful Imagination*, 34.

30. Sr. Marie Augusta Neal, *A Socio-theology of Letting Go* (New York: Paulist, 1977).

Index